The Leader That Society Did Not Choose

Vince Ford

TRILOGY CHRISTIAN PUBLISHERS

TUSTIN, CA

Trilogy Christian Publishers
A Wholly Owned Subsidiary of Trinity Broadcasting Network
2442 Michelle Drive
Tustin, CA 92780

For information, address Trilogy Christian Publishing

Rights Department, 2442 Michelle Drive, Tustin, Ca 92780.

Trilogy Christian Publishing/ TBN and colophon are trademarks of Trinity Broadcasting Network.

For information about special discounts for bulk purchases, please contact Trilogy Christian Publishing.

Manufactured in the United States of America

Trilogy Disclaimer: The views and content expressed in this book are those of the author and may not necessarily reflect the views and doctrine of Trilogy Christian Publishing or the Trinity Broadcasting Network.

10 9 8 7 6 5 4 3 2 1

Library of Congress Cataloging-in-Publication Data is available.

ISBN 978-1-64773-664-4
ISBN 978-1-64773-665-1 (ebook)

Track List

Dedication

Journeys are odd, it is interesting that it is even called a journey but that is exactly what the last seven years have been. God has steered this boat in this direction and although everything is a dedication to Him, I wanted to take this time to thank the people who have been instrumental in this book coming to fruition. I want to dedicate this book to my wife because she was the motivating factor behind bringing this idea to a reality. I must say that even with some of my wildest dreams she stands in support. You must dedicate great feats to people who instilled greatness in me. My mother never allowed us to strive for average, no matter what the activity, class, or job was, she demanded excellence. Mom, I hope this book is excellent for you.

To the Spiritual Hoodfellaz, I would not be able to do many of the things I do if it were not for you guys! Alvin, Carlos, and Johnathan I prayed for friends and God blessed me with brothers. To Brian Alexander, from diapers to dons, recognize a real one when you see one! You have been a brother that has always had my back since forever and for that I am grateful.

To Quincy, Stephen and Shawn I love you all and could not have been blessed with a better set of brothers! Finally, to my father, Vince Ford Sr. you have truly instilled in me what hard work means.

To my mother, Marshon Ford, you are a warrior not only for this country but for the Lord. I aspire to have your faith; I aspire to have your dedication and this book would not be possible if it were not for your vision. You told me, "You need to take the time during this pandemic and write a book." And I appreciate your encouragement. You worked countless jobs and still showed up for every game, every installation, your phone is always available for every tear and every laugh, and for that I dedicate this to you.

To my wife, Antwanelle, who would have thought that we would be here. You have stood by me and listened to my wildest dreams, laughed at my corniest jokes, and have brought three of the most wonderful boys in the world that I could ever ask for. Thank you for being by my side, this has been a journey. Since 2006, you have made an imprint on my heart that I will carry forever.

Foreword

Be a Leader

It is more than a pleasure to have the opportunity to lend my pen to one of the most important men in my life - my friend, and brother Vincent Lee Ford, II. Affectionately, I refer to my brother as "Vito". I have known Vito my entire life. Our parents attended Abilene Christian University together. We were born one month apart almost to the day in the city of Odessa, TX. Each year, we share a picture of us together as babies on our Facebook timelines to commemorate our bond. On his wedding day, when the photographer waived for the family to move towards the front of the church building for a picture I sauntered to the front as well. I planted my patented leather shoes in the space next to his mother at Vito's behest.

As we have both ascended into leadership roles, we've had to take turns celebrating and encouraging one another. As I write, I'm in the first year of being the principal of a high school. Vito was among the first to call and congratulate me. As I wrestled with how to manage the racial tension within the community where I work, I spoke with my brother frequently. His wisdom and ability to maintain perspective in complex situations have been invaluable to me.

Before my first day as a principal, Vito called to let me know that he was in the process of writing a book on leadership. My excitement for this undertaking could not be contained. To see his ministry extend beyond the pulpit and into the minds of those who would have never have met him personally, is beautiful. Well into his second decade of pulpit ministry and approaching the same marker in marriage, Vito has transformed from a student of the Bible to the embodiment of its contents. His words are, no doubt inspired, by the living God.

Just as the time of the early church, words given to the prophets, teachers, and preachers were not meant to be limited by geography. They are meant to strengthen, encourage, and guide the journey of those who seek His face. In particular, the contents of this book serve as means to reach those who seek a way to be an effective leader. It is difficult to describe what exactly makes someone an effective leader.

Commonly, people confuse being the boss with being a leader. It is important to know the difference. The position that one can hold within an organization makes one a boss. Managers, supervisors, appraisers, superintendents, and the like can all be referred to as being the "boss" within any given organization. Having a boss is critical to maintaining order within an organization. It is essential to the success of an organization for the proverbial buck to stop somewhere. Decisions must be made to promote the values and missions of an organization. It is the responsibility of the boss to do so. By nature, the title comes with a certain measure of power. Power and control are the two most valuable commodities within our mental space. Together, they are responsible for great happiness and great despair.

By the age of two, children have learned at least twenty words. The most widely used, from my experience, are "mommy" or "daddy", "no", and "mine". The last term, "mine" is our first introduction of the concept of control. Even before we truly understand the concept, we still seek the satisfaction of being able to determine the outcome of events. Being a boss or serving in a managerial role affords one the privilege of directly affecting the outcome.

In contrast, being a leader at times comes without the luxury of control. A leader is often thrust into circumstances that are out of their control. It was the responsibility of Moses to lead the children of Israel out of Egypt hundreds of years after they entered. In like fashion, leaders shoulder the unenviable task of assuming responsibility for events that were not caused by their actions.

In most situations, the only evidence of leadership is the lack thereof. The absence of leadership manifests itself in the spirit of their followers. An effective leader takes command of a situation in a way that their followers are neither alienated nor threatened by their own lack of control. Leaders create trust where there was none before. They are not bound to a title but tied to their followers through action.

In many cases, leaders were not selected by the people. This comes with its own set of challenges. Rejection from some is likely. However, effective leadership brings about positive change. As you read the words penned by my dear brother, I offer you these words: seek to be a leader - not a boss. The world is filled to brim with people who want to be in charge and in control. We are in desperate need of those who are charged to serve in situations where control is limited.

Know yourself. Know your worth.

Brian Alexander, M.Ed.

Prologue

In the same way, let your light shine before others, that they may see your good deeds and glorify your Father in heaven.
Matthew 5:16 (NKJV)

I wrote this book for two reasons. Number one, I hope that the church community can exercise grace and mercy on some of our leaders that have fallen victim to the same things that David fell victim to. Number two, I wrote this book for the young leader drinking from the proverbial fire hose but has a heart to serve God. Some might look at David as an instant success, nonetheless everything he went through from fighting Goliath, running from Saul, committing adultery, preparing Solomon to build a temple all are a part of his story, so that it could be our motivation. I wrote this book because no matter where you are in your ministry you are going through something that is going to require some exemplary leadership skills. Whether that is you are trying your best to serve at a church that does not appreciate you, or you are in a place in which problems and gossip grow faster than the weeds on the church lot. You might have just been let go unfairly, you might be walking into an assignment that looked great initially but now has turned into a warzone for you and your family, regardless of what is happening in your ministry right now, God expects us to be an example. Let your light shine, so that God gets the glory.

When God gets the glory, and He exalts us in due time we have no choice but to shine and shine bright. As a child living in Captain Marshon Ford's house, that is my mother who happens to be a captain in the US Army, she never let us settle for mediocrity. One of the worst things a leader can be is average. No one likes an average leader; football coaches get fired for going .500 year after year after year. I remember I would bring home a 95 percent on a quiz or test and my mother would praise my 95 but she would always say, "I need to you to understand that even if you got a 99 there is still 1 percent that you do not know". If leaders knew everything then leaders would not make mistakes, and the beauty of mistakes are the fact that mistakes teach us lessons and they are lessons to the people coming behind us. Truth be told the house I grew up in, 2106 Homestead Place, is the inspiration behind this book, everything I learned in that house is part of the reason I strive for leadership the way I do today.

2106 is the prefix to the house we moved into when I was seven years old. Looking back at it, I now realize how well we were doing because of the leadership skills of my parents. Our father spent thirty years with the police force and our mother was a school nurse and is a Captain in the US Army. There was a four-bedroom house with an office and a pool and a two-car garage. Unfortunately, my parent's marriage would end five years after we moved into that house. Nonetheless, the leadership and resilience of my mother prompted her to work countless jobs to ensure we always had a house to live in. As I dawn those doorsteps now, I cannot help but remember our mom removing the excuse of societal popularity and influence as a means of side-stepping leadership. We worked hard because hard work was the thing to do. Her infamous phrase was "You aren't at school for a likeable contest." Honestly, I had never heard of a likeable contest, I did not know it existed. That statement resonates with us even until this day, you can bet your life savings on the fact that if you are going through something on a job, at church, or with friends my mother will tell you, "Honey, you are not there for a likeable contest."

"What was a regular morning like at 2106?" Many would title those mornings as anything but normal. As four boys and a mom swiftly moved through each morning trying to conquer every new day, there was one thing consistently preached every morning and every night; this consistent sermon was leadership! Leadership in school, leadership in sports, leadership in society and most importantly; leadership in the church. Quite often my brothers and I would hear the infamous quote from our mother, "You are not at school for a likeable contest, and you are there to learn and to get an education. Don't you get your butt up there acting a fool, because I promise you, it will get ugly." As she looked each of us in the eyes with a piercing look of strength, we knew she was not playing games and if her orders were ignored there would be havoc to pay. These words sustain and inspire me to this day and because of the unrelenting dedication she provided within 2106, my brothers and I are sure we can be exactly who God has called us to be. So, what is leadership? Leadership is doing the right thing even if it hurts. Leadership is going the extra-mile, even if you have to go alone. Leadership is being a servant. Leadership is love for the less fortunate. Leadership is something anyone can be, no matter your skill, ability, or talent.

Stephen Ford Sr.

The ability to serve is the mastermind of your ability to lead. My mother would announce from the kitchen Vince-Quincy-Stephen-Shawn (all in one phrase), "One of y'all go get that book off my bed and read a little before you finish getting dressed." Understanding the value of a mother hearing her children read every morning was structured to continuous guidance by main source of leadership being able to serve. 2106 has molded a mindset of not allowing things to go undone and work while it is day. Developing the need for discipline disappears when you love what you do. Growing up in a rounded household, my brothers and I would subconsciously here the famous quote: "Y'all don't believe fat meat is greasy." Either prior to, or following the behavior that was not allowed in 2106. A law-abiding citizen in 2106 has taught me that I am the leader of my decisions, behaviors, and outcomes by the perception, demeanor, and character that we are individually displaying. So be mindful, be careful, be motivated, be loved, and know that great things are ahead.

Shawn Ford

Acknowledgement

Every person has people that they look toward for advice. My grandfather Willie Ford died in 2007 and my grandfather Arzell Jones about seven years later. I find it the most interesting that whenever I am in need of on-the-spot advice, I hear some of the things they would say in my head as I am pressing forward. Not a day goes by that I do not think about them. Often times, I find myself thinking about these men when I am in my office getting ready to preach or teach on a Sunday or Wednesday night. I remember one of my first sermons was videotaped and somehow my granddaddy Willie got a copy and my father would remind me that my grandfather would watch that tape very frequently, he would show it to friends that came over and hearing that was a solidifier that I was on the right path. There is something about the approval of your father, or a patriarch in your family. I remember as a high school football player my Dad sat in the same corner of the stands with sunglasses on no matter the time, and if I made a big play he was in that corner, if I made a horrible play he was in that corner and I want to thank my dad for always being in my corner.

The beauty of a fight, in which this life has had its fair share of fights, is the fact that while I'm in the ring, I know I have some people in my corner. I also want to acknowledge Mike Crosby who took a chance on a nineteen-year-old and let me tag along with you every day as an intern and expected me to preach at a nursing home every other Sunday like I was preaching in front of thousands of people. I believe that training prepared me for this pandemic, I believe that "no scrip, no lip" prepared me to attack every sermon with an expository mindset. Now let's take a trip to a small town in East Texas called Nacogdoches. There is a preacher there who made space for a young preacher like myself when I had no experience and saw something in me that at the time, I refused to see in myself. Those seven years in Nacogdoches was the spiritual formation I needed that helped me write this book. To Jesse Fogle, thank you sir, for everything you instilled in me.

Hip-Hop and Jesus

Let the word of Christ dwell in you richly in all wisdom; teaching and admonishing one another in psalms and hymns and spiritual songs, singing with grace in your hearts to the Lord.

Colossians 3:16 (NKJV)

You might ask why are the chapters listed as a track list like a rap album? It is simple, I love hip-hop. I am definitely thankful that hip-hop has been embraced as a genre that has infiltrated Christianity the way that it has. There are several Christian Hip-Hop artists that I listen to daily, and one thing that separates the good from the great is the same thing that separates the good authors from the great ones. Those lines of separation are lyrics, also known as words, in a book and flow, this book is the soundtrack to my ministry and I hope that it is inspiration to any young leader that is nestled deep in ministry and giving their entire life to it! This is one of the reasons I love David, because David had bars and

David was a musician. Today David would be heralded as one of the best rapper/producers of the day.

An Ode to the Leaders

In some regard, we are all leaders. You may be a leader on your job, a leader in your home, a leader in the community, or a leader of an organization or team. One of the beautiful aspects of leadership is the qualities are quite transitional. Another aspect of leadership is the people you are leading do not always have a choice in making you a leader. My children did not choose me as their father, but God chose me to lead them. I believe when we begin to look at our callings through the paradigm that we were chosen by God in this realm, I believe we will stand firm in our purpose and various callings. God chose me to be the husband to my wife, God chose me to be a servant in His church. With those choices, it is up to me to be mindful of what the responsibility is for me as a leader. There are times when God has expectations beyond the approval of society. Society does not always choose its leaders but that does mean that we can refrain from serving others because they do not support us. Jesus stood firm in His position of service to mankind regardless of if they were applauding Him or arresting Him, He knew what was at stake.

My question to you is do you know what is at stake? Are you aware of the generational implications that are at stake based on your leadership skills? One thing I want to leave you with exceedingly early, is mistakes are not the end of your purpose, sometimes it is the beginning of your Kingship. Sometimes it's the beginning of your Queenship. Even mistakes in the midst of your leadership does not mean it is over, the lesson learned if processed properly can provide us with a life changing lesson that can utterly change the trajectory of our life. There is not a leader in our modern world, or a leader historically besides Jesus Christ that did not have a life altering mistake or decision to make. Often times, the difference between legendary greatness and momently greatness is typically how we bounce back from the mistakes and the defeats we experience.

How does the story of David apply to leadership? When I first received this topic according to the theme for the year, I was a little worried it would apply. Then I began to reach out to some brothers in my circle, covenant brothers whom I trust, and the ideas began to pour. We are going to take a look at the ways we can reach the David's in our community. Many times, the people we least expect or the people we do not chose are the ones that God's chooses. With that in mind, it is important that we look at the heart of a human being rather than the social status, physical attributes, or their past. We can miss a number of people if we look at them from that scope of competencies. The more I looked at the story of David the more I saw myself. As I sit here in my office with two desks, both L shaped, one new and one old I realize that God put me here and no one else.

This was not on my radar, like David, he never had the goal of defeating Goliath, he tended his sheep and killed a bear and a lion along the way. That's the part that we have to begin to get people to dig into. Can they dig into their heart enough to find that bear and the lion moment that prepare them for Goliath? I did not go to seminary, I wanted to help my community, and I wanted to entrench myself in hip-hop, but Jesse Fogle and Jon Morrison saw something in me that encouraged them to encourage me. This is what evangelism is all about; you can build a relationship with someone that not only do they see that helps people see the presence of God, but they also allow someone to tap into their purpose that they may not have realized existed before that life changing moment.

When it comes to outreach, evangelism, and discipleship there should be steps attached to the process. Providing the outreach should lead to conversion which should lead to discipleship which should lead to being purpose driven. During these steps, the goal in multiplication should be attributing to the enhancement of leadership within the person's life. In some regard, we are all leaders, we may not have an official title at our place of worship, but many of us have families, siblings, and friends that look to us as an example of how to maneuver life. We are leading someone, and it should be the responsibility of all of us to lead people to Jesus. If being a leader is a surprise to some, just remember that being a Christian is a surprise to others for some people. The interesting thing about people is many times some of the victories we earn, and some of the decisions we make are a shock to them because typically people only view us within the box of our past. Similar to David, I'm certain that he was viewed as little brother, as a shepherd boy, similar to how we view our little brothers and sisters or people around us that lack experience or have never participated in the realm that they are now present in. This is the peculiar thing about experience, God makes the decisions on who leads. Even when you do not believe that you have attained the experience to step into Kingship or Queenship, just know God did not bring you this far just to drop you off.

Reaching the People that Society Did Not Choose

Think about playing pickup basketball on the court in middle school and not getting picked. Now you have a couple of options, you can watch everyone else play, or you can find something else to do. Aren't you glad that God does not operate like that? When He chooses you, it does not matter what everyone else says! He looked at Eliab and God said, "Nope, not the one." He looked at Shammah, it took seven good looks before He gets to the ruddy, handsome young man by the name of David.

That has to be a little frightening, you see all the military accomplishments and social accomplishments that your brothers have made, and now God has chosen you? So, think about how someone would feel hearing the gospel for the first time? Meanwhile, thinking of every reason they do not deserve salvation.

Let's really give a good look at this story. It was not just anyone who approached David's father, it was through the eyes of a prophet that still had to depend on the direction of God to make the right decision. This is why when God moves you to do something of anointing you must do it and trust that God is always going to make the right decision.

Unfortunately, we live in a society that takes physical appearance and attributes into such high consideration it is almost idolized. For instance, many of the presidents selected in this country have naturally been in good shape, taller men who typically have been identified with the United States population as good looking. We tend to make decisions based on assumptions physically, it's quite interesting God chose David. He wasn't the tallest man and based on the story of David and Goliath the armor of Saul was too large for him, so one could assume that he probably was not a very large man. Nonetheless, he became the giant slayer by trusting in God. I've always admired the unconventional route, it's truly a testament to who God is and how He has the ability to use anyone and anything for His will to be done. As it pertains to evangelism, biblically, God used a number of people from very unconventional backgrounds. The testimony of those who have been through things or society has turned their back on them, can serve as encouragement to those who are seeking God themselves. What we must be ready for is to allow God to use those not chosen by society to walk in their purpose, and even lead us to our place of refuge even if they do not look like the leader we envisioned. God did not choose David to slay Goliath, He choose him to slay Goliath so that he would become King.

When God Chooses the Young to Lead

It is interesting to note that although David was not the first pick by man, he was the anointed in the face of those who were looked upon by man to be of better choosing. David was anointed in the midst of his siblings. The further we read the more monumental this part of the story becomes. Considering we are on the brink of the challenge from Goliath, how his brothers and Saul treat him when he challenges Goliath is a warning sign.

I have been in a situation before in which my leadership skills were not embraced like I thought they should be. Everyone believes their ideas to be the best, right? Okay, only a few of us. Nevertheless, when I reflect on my first work, I could have been a lot more patient. I began my first work at the age of twenty-six years. My first Sunday in a pulpit as a Senior Minister was the day before my second son was born. When I arrived at the church, we had a consistent attendance of about eighty to one hundred people. From 2014 to 2016 our membership had tripled. We were truly reaching the unchurched. Young Adults were attending and serving in the community, we founded the Arizona State Youth Conference. Countless events for the community, and partnerships. To be honest, I was not on the radar of this church at all. A failed merger was the reason I was considered for the job in the first place. I remember preaching that Sunday evening and after a few months of serving as the youth minister we came to an agreement.

Again, I was only twenty-six, I had a young family, and I was a teacher during the day. I was chosen to lead, but I definitely had had a David and Saul moment with one of the Elders there who was very influential. I saw proverbial walls of defense come down if my message was soothing to his ears. From the outside looking in, it seemed like quite the work. Worship was vibrant, the praise was high! I had two brand new cars, a big home, and a beautiful family. Behind closed doors you would have thought God chose someone else.

As we were planning for 2016, every plan that I had put together was met with disdain. A marriage conference that we had scheduled eighteen months out was cancelled while I was at a speaking engagement out of the state. Finally, the rubber met the road one fateful night after prayer service. Earlier that day we had a knockout drag out meeting, my frustration was so high I wanted to just stand up in the meeting and say I quit. I did not quit but they handled the exit for me. Little did I know a vote had been taken a few weeks back without my knowledge from the elders and a few ministry leaders to move forward without me. After prayer service one of the Elders decided it was the right time in which he told me they would be going in a different direction. Here I am with a young family, in the weeks to come I would have to return cars, move out of my house, and live in a hotel for approximately three weeks. It would have been four, but thanks be to the son of my mentor who allowed us to stay with him until we found an apartment. That was my Goliath moment. During this time, the church I served as youth minister at was going through a Goliath moment as well. As it turns out, the minister they had decided to resign. Be mindful that when you show up to slay a Goliath that the soldiers there are afraid to challenge, they will discredit your faith. Regardless of your public anointing, regardless of your calling people will always have an opinion until the giant falls!

Here is the important part, understanding the next step after the giant falls. What are your next steps after the heralding wears off, after the clapping is over? Now there is work to do. The biggest thing you can do is add strategy to your victory. Too many times have I seen too many young leaders relishing over the recent victory of yesterday. The sermon with a huge number of responses, the Sunday with multiple baptisms and memberships placed, the great event with huge turnout. Those things are great but when those things are over your own backyard still needs tending to. Also, remember everyone is not happy that you are in a place of influence.

Saul hurled the spear for he thought, "I will pin David to the wall." But David escaped from his presence twice. Now Saul was afraid of David, for the Lord was with him but had departed from Saul.[1]

1 Samuel 18:11-12 (NASB)

Be mindful that Saul lost his influence and power, Saul did not have anyone to blame but himself. Nonetheless, when we are not happy with an outcome and want to justify ourselves and refuse to hold ourselves accountable, we find someone to blame. Saul could not blame Samuel, he was the Prophet, he was a messenger of God. Here we are with a new King, ruddy in appear-

---

1 *New American Standard Bible: 1995 update.* (1995). (1 Sa 18:11–12). La Habra, CA: The Lockman Foundation.

ance as the Bible tells us, a shepherd, the one that was overlooked. Now Saul is, for a lack of better terms Salty (Saulty). I might just use that as a term to endear older leaders who stifle the growth of younger leaders, instead of helping them reach new heights. Stop being so "Saulty!" Think about this for a few moments. Imagine if Saul had taken David in, considering Jonathan and David are best friends. It could have prompted itself to be the greatest story of transition ever. Notwithstanding the drama that ensues, it became a measure of what not to do, and a measure of what I have experienced and seen as a young preacher in the brotherhood.

Understand that before David is running from Saul, he was ministering to the spirit of Saul.

Now the Spirit of the Lord departed from Saul, and an evil spirit from the Lord terrorized Saul's servants then said to him, "Behold now, an evil spirit from God is terrorizing you. "Let our lord now command your servants who are before you. Let them seek a man who is a skillful player on the harp; and it shall come about when the evil spirit from God is on you, that he shall play the harp with his hand, and you will be well." So, Saul said to his servants, "Provide for me now a man who can play well and bring him to me." Then one of the young men said, "Behold, I have seen a son of Jesse the Bethlehemite who is a skillful musician, a mighty man of valor, a warrior, one prudent in speech, and a handsome man; and the Lord is

with him." So, Saul sent messengers to Jesse and said, "Send
me your son David who is with the flock." [2]

1 Samuel 16:14–19 (NASB)

Some predecessors can only love you in a subor-
dinate role. It's quite discouraging that this happens.
Looking at this verse, the Bible tells us a few things. David is skillful, and he is described as a mighty man of
valor, prudent in speech, and the Lord was with him.
In the development of leaders, you have to be mindful
and accepting of the fact that the talent of the person
you are developing might be greater than what you pos-
sess. I think of NFL coaches like Tony Dungy, who is
singlehandedly responsible for providing a lane of Afri-
can American Coaches over the past fifteen years. One
of the coaches in his coaching tree is Mike Tomlin, who
has had more success as a coach than Dungy has had,
I believe he has won more games and been in a head
coach role longer. Tony Dungy was able to develop men,
because Dennis Green believed in him. Honestly, many
of us are only as successful as the people that poured
into us. It's quite odd when these tables turn amongst
the people you have been leading. I remember it was
reported once that as Mason Rudolph was drafted by
the Steelers, someone asked Ben Roethlisberger if he

2 *New American Standard Bible: 1995 update.* (1995). (1 Sa 16:14–
19). La Habra, CA: The Lockman Foundation.

was going to mentor the new quarterback drafted. He essentially responded that if [he] Mason Rudolph asked a question; he would just point to the playbook.

We all have a playbook, if you are in ministry the Bible is definitely our playbook, but the problem is using the playbook as a tool of defense or certainty has caused many young leaders to lose jobs, influence, or walk around with the proverbial target on their back. Young leaders, I will contend that right is right no matter what. You have to ask yourself is your integrity worth less than a paycheck? The old adage, you can do one hundred things right and someone will hold one of those over your head forever. Impressing people will lead you down a long road of frustration and grief. God did not call you to lead his people from a place of impression. If you look at many biblical leaders one of the things you will see is the fact that people were very upset with some of their decisions. People were upset with Moses, Noah, Jesus, Paul, Peter, Amos, Haggai, Hezekiah and many other men inspired by God's word.

You Have Been Chosen to Lead, Now What?

2 Samuel 5 gives us an inside look at how David handles his new responsibilities. Before we get into how new responsibilities should be handled, one thing we must know is whomever has passed you the torch you will be compared to them. I am not saying you should mimic or become a carbon copy of your predecessor, nor should you fall into the trap of listening to all the damaging decisions they made and try to be a polar opposite. The best thing you can do is be unapologetically yourself. In my first Senior Pastor role I found myself operating outside of the realm of who Vincent truly was. I believe if I had been me from the beginning, I could have avoided a lot of heartache. The blessing is I learned so much about myself during the first three years, it has shaped ministry for me in a totally differ-

ent way. This is why I admire David, his ability to reflect in the moment and call upon the name of God. Calling on God is something that you must do constantly and consistently in any leadership position. There are things that I innately do that remind people of the minister before me, and there are times in which people will begin a suggestion by referencing how things were done aforetime. You have to find your way to create a platform so that the people are aware that it comes from you but that it is for the best interest of the people you are pastoring in the moment.

When we think about leaders in the Bible, we see a number of leaders who constantly rely on their conversation with God to see them through. We also see instances in which the pastoral responsibility of these leaders causes them to reach out on behalf of those they are leading.

Then Moses returned to the Lord and said, "Oh, these people have committed a great sin, and have made for themselves a god of gold! Yet now, if You will forgive their sin—but if not, I pray, blot me out of Your book which You have written."
Exodus 32:31-12 (NKJV)

Moses asks for forgiveness on their behalf, but his trust in God allows him to be content with the decision that God makes. It is a tough situation to see the people whom you are serving go through various, trials and consequences. Our response has to be consistent conversation with God, and strength to turn that conversation into life changing teaching that is profitable to the entire body of Christ.

Leadership is difficult when the tragedy hits close to home. Abraham pleaded with God on behalf of Sodom and Gammorah, and I assume it is because his nephew and his nephew's family were residents in the city of Sodom. This conversation with God is one that must continue at all times. Praying without ceasing should quite honestly be in your job description because any effort in ministry, especially leadership, is going to require an intimate relationship with God!

Constantly Remember that God Chose You!

I often wonder if I had been in this situation, would I have stayed resilient enough to bid my time for the throne? David was anointed by Samuel, in the midst of waiting for his chance to be king, he was faced with a bitter king. Saul was upset that his kingship is about to come to an end, and he made attempts on David's life. David, while ministering to Saul with his harp, must dodge a spear that is aimed for his head.

God choosing you does not mean that you will not embrace hardship. I wonder would kind of king would David had been had he not went through his issues with Saul? I often believe that it is hard to appreciate anything, when there was no work attached to it. Do we assume that if God chose us it should be easy? We have to remember that if God chose us, that the enemy wants to destroy us. If he can destroy us, and remove us, detach us, or separate us from our God intended purpose. If we are separated, Satan wins. David had to remember he was chosen even when he caught Saul slipping and could have ended his life. His conscious stepped in after he removed a piece of his garment. When we are anointed by God, His spirit steps in and we find ourselves doing things we would not have normally done. Do not dismiss the spirit that is attached to your appointed anointment. Throughout all the mistakes, throughout all the heartaches and the pain, God still has a purpose for your life.

Our purpose should align with God. No matter the circumstance, God gets the glory, and your purpose is reinforced. Your purpose should shine on your job, your purpose should shine amongst your friends. David did not stop being king when he was around certain people, he was still anointed, even when he had to stand alongside the Philistines after being forced to live in Ziklag for over a year. Location does not determine purpose, age does not determine purpose, and your circumstances do not determine your purpose. Your purpose is God driven, God designed, and God appointed.

Your purpose always has to be God driven. When you are in a leadership position, you begin to love the people that you are serving. When you love people, sometimes your heart can get in the way of what God is trying to do. Especially, when you are a person with vision. You do not just see a church, you see a resource for the community, you do not just see an empty plot of land you see you a transitional housing space for people transitioning out of foster care for 180 days. Okay, that is my vision, sorry I went off on a tangent, but nonetheless, where you are might not be where your greatest successes come true. A God driven purpose does not mean you are just sitting passenger side idly; you are truly seeking God in everything you do. It is similar to following someone in a car, when they switch lanes you switch lanes, when they brake you brake, when they turn, you turn. God being the leader of our lives treats us like a great navigator of traffic. He turns the blinker on earlier than need be to let us know when our life is about to take a turn, He allows life to slow down when we need to take a different route. Even though you may have an idea of the way to get there, still trust God's instructions.

Our purpose is God designed. Considering it is God designed, we must first remember as the writer of Ephesians exclaimed, "We are God's handiwork." We are designed for good works; these instances are not happenstance. God created us in His own image, for a specific purpose. My mother has this uncanny ability to help people. She also is never frightened by not knowing how to do something. Her job in our community is a nurse, she has worked as a school nurse for over twenty-five years. She's also a nurse in the US Army Reserves and is currently deployed. She is a mother of four boys, and she referees basketball and volleyball. All those things are jobs, but her purpose is helping people. She's helped people in Guyana, Honduras, America, and Kuwait. She's had conversations with young men and women who wanted to give up, and our house was always open. There were many of mornings I would wake up and see one of my buddies laying on the couch because they had nowhere else to go. Her purpose is helping people, God has designed that purpose to be manifested through nursing, refereeing, and opening her home.

Do you believe that God puts you in the places He needs you to be and not where you want to be? I did not realize the purpose of being in Arizona until we left. Initially, my wife wanted to build a life in Texas. I had lived in Texas all my life and wanted something new. I had been preaching in an assistant role and I was perfectly fine with that. I taught Bible class on Sunday mornings and that was enough for me. When we moved to Phoenix, considering everything that I went through personally and in ministry, where I am today, the journey in Phoenix was a preparation for all these moments. One of the hardest things to wrap your mind around, is the fact that where you are right now may not even be for nothing else but preparation for the next move.

David was anointed but he did not have his appointment yet. One of the toughest things to deal with as a man is knowing you are chosen but the door has not opened just yet. We have to remember that God opens door, if we have to kick a door in, we have to ask ourselves are we supposed to be in the room? It's an interesting perspective seeing someone rise to the occasion when society did not choose them, their family did not choose them, and now they have to convince the people closest to them that God chose them. David's brother, so distraught by Goliath, was upset when David brought food down to support the troops.

"Now Eliab his oldest brother heard when he spoke to the men; and Eliab's anger was aroused against David, and he said, "Why did you come down here? And with whom have you left those few sheep in the wilderness? I know your pride and the insolence of your heart, for you have come down to see the battle."

1 Samuel 17:28 (NKJV)

Sometimes even family does not want you in their realm. David was only following instructions from his

3 *The New King James Version.* (1982). (1 Sa 17:28). Nashville: Thomas Nelson.

father; his brother could not see that because of the overarching fear of Goliath. Then he even attempted to be concerned by asking about the sheep. If that's not enough, we then see Eliab take a jab at the character of David by labeling him prideful and insolent. David came to serve, not to be a spectator. Everyone at the front row seat of your trial is not always there to spectate defeat, but to serve you at the request of someone else. We have to be able to know the difference. It is difficult in the moment of fear to see clearly what people are truly doing for you. This was a danger to David as well. The beautiful thing that this passage does is give us an inside view at the courage and dependability that David has on God.

Then David says something that will stick with me for the rest of my life, "Let no man's heart fail because of him". If you end up quitting, do not let it be because someone is doubting you. No matter how much success you end up achieving there will always be doubters. I remember during Barack Obama's presidency; this man had been re-elected and there were still people heralding insults such as the legitimacy of his citizenship in the United States. Think about that for a moment, a man who is the leader of the free world is being doubted. Doubt is a part of the process, church members will doubt decisions, leadership teams do not always agree; but we have to remain steadfast in our calling to leadership no matter our age and no matter the size of the enemy.

We must get to a place in which we refrain from even recognizing negativity by name. Instead we must call on the name of God. "God will deliver me," an iconic phrase in this story but it carries much validity when we are faced with trials. We have to realize, believe, and convey that if God is almighty, creator, and loving He will deliver us in our time of need.

How to Handle Goliath Moments

By now, in ministry I imagine you have had your Goliath moment. Often times, this is why churches entrust you with leading them because they want someone who will stare the proverbial Goliath in the face. Here's the tough part for young ministers, you have been anointed and appointed but influence is still not there. Influence takes time, the Pastor Emeritus may not be speaking to the people every Sunday anymore but there is a historical influence that they are measuring you up to. While you are building your own influence, lean on the Man of God that labored there before you prior to your existence.

Spend time with Him, talk with Him, and gain insight some from. Paul told Timothy to entreat the older men as Fathers. This was a difficult lesson to learn my first appointment as Senior Minister in Phoenix, Arizona. After much conversation and talking to a counselor, it was determined that a lot of the resentment I had for older men was rooted in the relationship that me and my father had. My parents split when I was twelve years old. Instantly at the age of twelve, I became the next dependable line of defense after my mother. I cooked for my brothers, helped with homework, and even worked to help my mom pay bills. This gave me a sense of manhood and power that prompted me to walk in a room full of older men and equate myself with them. I also believed they could not tell me anything that I did not already know. I also had this complex that if I was right and it would help, we should go along with it. What I had not realized is that the generations ahead of us cannot help but to look at a twenty-six-year-old minister like a son. It is not to say that I just let everything go and do what they say, but it was to say that I considered their insight and knew it was a matter of time before it was my time. One thing you cannot refrain from doing is spending time with the next generation in effort to develop leaders during your tenure. David was not on the throne forever; Solomon was coming and there is preparation that has to be in place in effort to solidify the future.

Goliath moments will bring about a sense of encouragement and a sense of hate and frustration from others. Saul was not a happy man when he returned home to hear them sing the praises of David. Everyone is not going to be happy about your success. Often times, you do not realize how unhappy people are with your success until you infringe on their influence. One of the most intimidating things in the church today is influence. Influence is the reason why people ask you to mediate family disputes, and why they tell you that there is no toilet paper in the women's bathroom. I imagine you have a person over facilities and you probably have someone in the pews who is a licensed family therapist but for some reason because your sermon speaks to their spirit, they'll come to you. The obscure thing about influence is there is someone who is glad they are coming to you and then there are those who wish they would come to them. Finding balance and being observant enough to delegate when necessary, and meet the need when necessary.

These are the defining factors of overcoming Goliath moments. David had to know when to minister to Saul. David also had to know when to defer to Jonathan and Michal. Goliath moments do not always only happen once, I believe they change form. He defeated Goliath, but then Goliath turned into Saul, Goliath turned into the Amalekites, Goliath turned into bouncing back after his adultery with Bathsheba and the murder of her husband. One giant falling does not mean that more giants are not on the way. The strategies might change but the giant still has to be slain. The consult to gain a good strategy has to be God, regardless of the type of giant God has to be the go-to. Often times, we want to defeat Goliath the same way our friends did, our pastor did, or even our parents. Your Goliath may take a different strategy, remember the strategy given by Saul to David? David responds with the notion that I cannot wear your armor to defeat this Giant. You might even be slaying the giant for other people but the way you slay the giant has to be authored by God.

When Enemies Become Friends

The spirit and the willingness of being helpful is not always well received. Some people want the job done, but they just do not want you to do it. The other side of that coin is many people who do not mind helping do not care who does the job they just want the job to get done. Fear brings out some emotions in people that will make you question the entirety of their character. Here is the handful of encouragement; you have to be okay with not being a hero to everybody. If you listen to hip-hop like I do or watch superhero movies you probably remember this quote. Aaron Eckhart plays Harvey Dent and as he is sitting at the table he says, "You either die a hero or you live long enough to see yourself become a villain." Jay-Z utters the same sentiment in which the lyrics go, "Dark Knight feeling, die and be a hero, or live long enough to see yourself become the villain." As long as you are in leadership you will transition between beloved hero, vigilante, and sometimes unpopular villain. This is why it is so important that above you listen to God. Search the scriptures diligently and pray as much as you possibly can. Your closeness to God is not going to keep people from disliking you and discrediting you. God has the power to lead you in the midst of enemies and naysayers. "Lead me, O Lord, in Your righteousness because of my enemies; Make Your way straight before my face."[4] (Psalm 5:8, NKJV) You need the guidance because of your enemies, but God blesses you and makes your way straight in spite of your enemies. One of the most confusing things for the enemy is blessings amidst trial. When they are doing everything, they possibly can to derail your journey. Sometimes people are looking out for that would never anticipate cared about you one bit.

I was raised by an ex-college football all conference safety, turned police office, who found pride in working out with high school and college athletes while I was playing football. I do not think my dad really stopped lifting weights heavily until after I graduated high school. My father was the epitome of teaching, "If someone hits you, you better hit them back or I'm gonna hit you." In middle school I was good at football, I was also very strong for my age. I also wore these big round

---

4 *The New King James Version*. (1982). (Ps 5:8). Nashville: Thomas Nelson.

glasses, had inconsistent haircuts, crooked teeth and my wardrobe looked like it came straight out of 1990's R&B video. So, it's safe to say I got picked on regularly. Well, in the eighth grade in particular, I was still getting picked on but I started to come into my own, had a little more say so with clothes but there was this guy who was gang affiliated that would not leave me alone. Every day he would just pick and pick and pick.

One day during transition it was just me, and one of my closest buddies at the time, Drew Norwood and bunch of his friends. I did not know he was in the bathroom until he pushed me while I was trying to use to the restroom at the urinal. Basically, he told me that day either I was going to fight or get beat up, but I was not leaving the bathroom without the fight. He pushed me and he knocked my glasses off, I handed them to my friend Drew and the fight began, honestly I blacked out, I came to as my football coach Fred Parker grabbed me by my collar as I had this young man's head in the toilet as I was punching him. I was a hero amongst my peers that day, but a villain to his friends.

Well, a few days later, I'm walking home and police officers grabbed me and placed me in the back of a squad car. My mother picked me up from school and says, "Thank God the girl you sit by in math told the teachers they were going to jump you, because those young men had steel pipes and razors on them." Now the young lady that told the teachers was not a friend, she was actually a friend of the people that were going to jump me, but because I was always friendly to her in class, she did not want that to happen to me.

You never know who is looking out for you. Yet, on the other end of things there were people who were actually jealous that I fought the bully. Nonetheless, they had the respect and influence to derail his attempts to picking on me. Just like David, Saul wanted to provide armor for David when he was unsure that he could slay Goliath but once he defeated the Giant, he wanted to kill him. Listen, God provides you with what you are anointed to have; God will appoint you in due time. Sometimes, people are upset that you were chosen to do something they were afraid to do in the first place. Just do not allow their bitterness to discourage you from doing exactly what you were called to do. You can control your ability to obey God and answer His call, but you cannot control how people will respond to who God calls. Granted, David did not want to be on the run from Saul, if it had not been for Saul, David would have never gained Jonathan as a friend even more so a brother.

Your Assignment Can Change Once You Arrive to Where You Have Been Sent

Have you ever gone somewhere with one intention and left completing a different task? This is what happened to David. I am reminded of what my old principal, Lisa Norwood would tell us as teachers when we were upset that the plan, we had in place could not be carried out. "Monitor and adjust," she would say when she walked into my classroom as I was wasting the learning time of my students because my project was not working. Although I wanted to teach from PowerPoint, or show a video the longer I tinkered with that projector the less my students would learn. So, if it meant for that day I wrote vocabulary words from our section on

Civil Rights, that is what I had to do to ensure that my students left better than when they came into the classroom. David was sent by his father to tend to the sustenance needs of his brothers and other soldiers who were fighting for the valued freedoms of living as God's chosen people. Nonetheless, when David got to where his brothers were the assignment had changed. Ministry works in a similar way, you go on the interview, you meet your staff, you are hired, and you have all of these elaborate plans. Once you get knee deep in the assignment, you realize that as much as you envisioned outreach evangelism taking off year one, there are so many families that are hurting, there are people getting divorced, there are people from losing loved ones and as much as you came with the intent to share the gospel with the neighborhood there's some Goliath's within the four walls that need to be dealt with.

Everyone's Protection Plan Will Not Grant You Victory

Have you ever asked a friend some advice and halfway through the conversation you think to yourself, *why did I even ask?* Sometimes the way people emotionally and spiritually protect themselves is not the way that you will eventually protect yourself. We have to be cognizant of the idea that our ability and protection has to come from God, but how we apply it to our lives may look different. Even with armor on that belonged to Saul, David still had God's protection. Nonetheless, when God is on my side, I can use what I'm accustomed to in effort to get a similar result. God was not looking for another soldier he was looking for another King. It's no coincidence He allowed an unconventional method to be the determining factor in defeating a giant that everyone else was afraid of.

Let's think about this for a second. You come down to check on your siblings who are at a place in a battle in which they cannot retreat but are too afraid to attack. They get upset with you for checking on them, they accused you of getting a first-class seat to their demise. You try on the leader's armor, you find out it does not fit, you use what you have and now you are the hero. Life moves like this, often times was seems like an overnight success is years and years of dedication and hard work. This same David had slain a bear and a lion. Granted Goliath, based on historical compubox numbers (sorry I'm a boxing fan), listed at nine feet, incredible reach and avenger strength probably seemed to be a tougher opponent than a bear. Nonetheless, the ability to move without fear because you know God is on your side is a nice tool to have in your toolbox.

The best tool you can have in your toolbox is God! There are plenty of tools out there, podcast, self-help books, friends, but there is no greater tool than God. I believe these other things are great supplements, but faith is your greatest asset and trust in God is your most lethal weapon in dealing with uncertainty. What we seek during trouble reflects what we prioritize in life. *Seek ye first* has to be a mindset that is applied to all walks of life. David did not get to a place in which

God coined him a man after His own heart because he put God second. Again, supplemental material is very good to have, fine, and it can be quite beneficial, but they should never be prioritized over God. Some extracurriculars will give advice that does not work for everyone. For instance, many people are trying to lose weight and they follow Instagram models and fitness gurus and become frustrated when the plan that they provided does not work for their body. The reason being is because everything does not work for everyone. For instance, a year ago I weighed three hundred and forty pounds. I played sports for majority of my life, so I knew what working out looked like. I know my way around a gym and can lift weights with ease. My issue was my eating habits, I had not found a plan that worked for me. I had tried all sorts of dieting plans and it was not until I prayed about my fitness and sought out a professional that I began to see the results I had dreamed of.

It's a similar story when Saul bestows David with his armor, armor that he was afraid to fight Goliath in, an armor that would have brought him defeat. The difference with David is that his faith allows him to prioritize God in this moment of obstacle. David was no novice to life threatening situations. He had slayed extremely dangerous animals protecting the sheep that he was a shepherd of.

But David said to Saul, "Your servant used to keep his father's sheep, and when a lion or a bear came and took a lamb out of the flock, 35 I went out after it and struck it, and delivered the lamb from its mouth; and when it arose against me, I caught it by its beard, and struck and killed it.⁵

1 Samuel 17:34–35 (NKJV)

My mindset would be okay with David taking a proverbial stab at Goliath considering killing a Lion and Bear are nothing to sneeze at but this arena was foreign to David according to his three brothers and the king that were standing on the sidelines of battle that was supposed to be taking place. You hear the prioritization of God in David's life with this statement

"The Lord, who delivered me from the paw of the lion and from the paw of the bear, He will deliver me from the hand of this Philistine."⁶

1 Samuel 17:37 (NKJV)

The focus and the dependability on God was where David's mind was. You can see this by his response, he does not attribute his victory over the lions to his strength, he positions his deliverance within the hands

---

5 *The New King James Version.* (1982). (1 Sa 17:34–35). Nashville: Thomas Nelson.
6 *The New King James Version.* (1982). (1 Sa 17:37). Nashville: Thomas Nelson.

of God. This testimony gives enough confidence in Saul that he would give David his armor. I do not know about you, but I am not entrusting my armor with anyone who does not have some experience that I can buy into. Nonetheless, I would be remiss if I did not believe that I thought Saul had faith in David's ability to defeat this giant.

So, Saul clothed David with his armor, and he put a bronze helmet on his head; he also clothed him with a coat of mail. 39 David fastened his sword to his armor and tried to walk, for he had not tested them. And David said to Saul, "I cannot walk with these, for I have not tested them." So, David took them off.[7]

1 Samuel 17:38–39 (NKJV)

Testing them meant he had not taken careful investigation of the armor. Sometimes the armor of others can do more damage to what you are attempting to accomplish. I can admire the workout of a body builder, I even admire the workout of my trainer, Juan, but there are exercises that he can do that I would injure myself badly if I attempted to try.

It is alright to turn down the "armor" of other people, even if they are the king of that realm. Just make

---

7 *The New King James Version.* (1982). (1 Sa 17:38–39). Nashville: Thomas Nelson.

sure you follow up your rejection with something you have expertise in. David had the sling shot and smooth stones on his person as if it was something that he carried with him everywhere. We know that he did not take the slingshot and stones because he had intentions of fighting Goliath because his purpose for going to check on his brothers was to bring them food, not help them win the fight. Remember, what you are an expert in is something you are carrying with you right now. You may not have any intention of going to battle but God's preparation works in that way. Even with my preaching style and my teaching style, God gifted me with confidence to speak in front of people long before I even stepped into a pulpit. I remember being given the armor of style and cadence, that I would attempt to put on, but they would never work for me. I had to use the slingshot that God had given me in my pasture. As unconventional as a slingshot is for war, when victory happens typically no one cares what has been used they just know it worked. Historically, we find ancient Egyptian paintings and depictions of Assyrian soldiers that would have used a similar instrument during war times as early as 800 B.C.

David would have been depicted as brave and fearless had he used Saul's armor to fight Goliath. Imagine if he had lost, there would be no kingship, no Solomon, no various triumphs, or a 23rd Psalm. We would know

David as the young shepherd boy who put his life on the line for his family and his nation. Right now there is something that you are being called to do, and once you arrive at your destination you will receive doubt and potentially walk into the giant of your life, but do not worry because the same God that protected you from the lions and bears of your life, is going to protect you in the face of Goliath. Remember you can turn down Saul's armor especially if you have not tested them yet. Everyone's advice does not work for everyone. Your mentor can be wrong, your parents can be wrong, your friends with more experience can be wrong. Remain assertive and use what God put in your pocket on the way up to check on your brothers.

Now I am not saying that you should not heed healthy advice, but do not just accept the advice if you haven't tested it yet. What does testing look like? Testing, or trying on, or simply being assertive about the fact that this does not work for you. I believe that we can get caught up in accepting "armor" because we value the experience and position of the people offering these protections to us. Imagine if David took the armor and was heralded as a martyr but would have never had the impact as king. He may not have ever had the friendship or brotherhood that he had with Johnathan. There is nothing wrong with being a martyr, nonetheless David's ability to step out on faith shows his trust in God even during a life or death circumstances.

Do Let the Noise of Fans Distract You

So here we are, Goliath is dead. You have defeated your giant. This is a good feeling, but this is where the work really starts. As David continues to rise in popularity, we hear this historical song that is sang by the residents in this town. It is evident through the reading of scripture that Saul resents David and even attempts to kill him. David has the support of the people but the most powerful man in the land wants his head on a platter. This is the tough part about upstaging decision makers, often before they ever process how it would make them feel if you were successful, it is typically too late. Our issue is typically we do not expect people to be as successful as we initially thought. Once you have your victory, especially a victory that no one believed that you would have, everyone is not going to be happy.

On the other hand, do not lose sight because people cheer for you. You will have people in your corner but understand that it is popular to be in the corner of the champion. I am reminded of Mike Tyson, who became the youngest heavyweight champion ever in the history of boxing. When he was the champion it seemed like everyone was his friend, but when life took a turn for the worse, a lot of people distanced themselves. You will get championship parades when you defeat Goliath and win battles for wars but you will also have times of anguish in which you feel like God is not listening to you and you are all alone. This is what life brings to us, it is filled with ups and downs. The key is to always be mindful of the people that mourn with you and the people that celebrate with you. The confusing part about your circle is when you have to differentiate between people who actually want to mourn with you versus the people who cannot handle the celebration because they really did not want to see you win.

I remember when my family was struggling during my period of unemployment it was a few people that were there during the struggle that would not even return calls when opportunities came, and our situation became better. We really must be mindful of what people's intentions are. Saul was okay as long as David was ministering to him, but once the spirit of envy helped him come back to his feelings of resentment, he would do things like throw a spear at the head of his successor. One thing I have told my son since we have moved is that friendships have to work both ways, you can put in as much effort as you want, but if the other party is not willing to show love or build a formidable relationship it does not matter. Vulnerability comes when we feel safe, seen, and heard. Saul had no intentions of helping David feel comfortable because his kingship was coming to an end. Take a second to sit back and ask yourself how people around react to my success? How does my mentor react to my success? Constructive criticism and the encouragement to remain humble are healthy, but if people who you deem as mentors, friends, and even family are passive aggressive about your passions it may be time to reevaluate the relationship.

So, the women sang as they danced, and said:
"Saul has slain his thousands,
And David his ten thousands."
Then Saul was very angry, and the saying displeased him; and he said, "They have ascribed to David ten thousands, and to me they have ascribed only thousands. Now what more can he have but the kingdom?"[8]

1 Samuel 18:7–8 (NKJV)

---

8 *The New King James Version.* (1982). (1 Sa 18:7–8). Nashville: Thomas Nelson.

As we can see in this text, ego is coming in to play. David is young, popular and the women are singing and dancing for him. This is like cheerleaders on the sideline and they cheer for you when you score but they cheer louder when the new young player scores. It's ironic that this happens following Saul's disobedience, so his spirit of uncertainty was probably overwhelming at the time. There were many things that Saul did that were irrational. From calling on the medium to get in contact with Samuel, or him attempting on many occasions to try to kill David. The unsettling feelings in Saul's life and his broken ego was not a recipe for success between him and David.

10And it happened on the next day that the distressing spirit from God came upon Saul, and he prophesied inside the house. So, David played music with his hand, as at other times; but there was a spear in Saul's hand. 11 And Saul cast the spear, for he said, "I will pin David to the wall!" But David escaped his presence twice.12 Now Saul was afraid of David, because the Lord was with him, but had departed from Saul.[9]

1 Samuel 18:10–12 (NKJV)

David had the popularity; David had built a beautiful friendship with the son of the current king, but this

---

9 *The New King James Version.* (1982). (1 Sa 18:10–12). Nashville: Thomas Nelson.

spirit of distress and selfishness caused Saul to want to take his life. Saul was threatened by the success of David, the ability to claim victory over a giant that Saul was afraid to fight. His ego was bruised by the noise in the stands from the women who acclaimed that David had done more. The fans in the stands can have a distracting effect or a discouraging effect. Therefore, you do not need to be driven by what the people in the stands are saying. We are in service of the audience of one, and that is God. Saul essentially brough this on himself through disobedience which led to his direction but when we do not want to be held accountable for our actions. Nonetheless, be mindful of the fact that you need to remain focused, the people may love you but those in close proximity to you might be trying to destroy you.

Knock the Giant Down then Cut Off the Head

In life we cannot leave room for the giants in life to get back up. There are temptations, challenges, and obstacles that must be knocked down and cut off. Sometimes the challenges rest inside of us, sometimes the greatest Goliath we will face is ourselves. It is not secret that our biggest nightmare can be us. One of the great things about a surprising task that you did not think you would have to deal with is having to decide in the moment. There was no anticipation, it was simply that David showed up, David felt compelled, and David acted. The ironic thing about these situations is that they are a testament to where our focus is and who we really are. David knows he is going to an area that might be a little more dangerous than the pasture with the sheep, nonetheless, his father believes it's safe enough to send him to attend to the physical need by bringing food.

In football there is this term that analysts, coaches, and even players use when they were winning a game and a team comes back to win in the final moments of what could have been an upset. They call it "hanging around". At halftime when I played football, my coach would say, "We have them right where we want the now it's time to break their necks." A violent term, I know, but challenges as such are often violent circumstances. I am always reminded of Coach Denny Green when the Cardinals lost by one point to the Bears. They had forced a number of turnovers against Rex Grossman and the Chicago Bears and ended up losing by one point. Coach Green emphatically explains to the reporters that "They were who we thought they were, and we let them off the hook." Sometimes, we are so surprised to be in the lead against Goliath we do not know how to finish the job. For David in this instance, this was a realm of war and David knew if Goliath had the opportunity, he was going to kill David. The enemy has no intentions of shaking your hand after battle, his goal is to end your life right where you stand.

"31 And the Lord said, "Simon, Simon! Indeed, Satan has asked for you, that he may sift you as wheat. "[10]

Luke 22:31 (NKJV)

---

10 *The New King James Version.* (1982). (Lk 22:31). Nashville: Thomas Nelson.

David understood this, therefore after he connected with the smooth stones from the sling shot, the next step in victory was cutting off the head of the giant. I know this sounds quite violent in nature, but in retrospect the enemy is looking to do the same thing to us.

If he is able to fight with me and kill me, then we will be your servants. But if I prevail against him and kill him, then you shall be our servants and serve us."[11]

1 Samuel 17:9 (NKJV)

Goliath brought this on himself, nonetheless, it was victory and death. Otherwise, the people of God would have been in bondage to the Philistines. "Fight with me and kill me" was the arrangement. I need you to understand right now that in this fight we call life there is no standing eight count, no three-knockdown rule, whomever wins knows that their life is on the line. I believe if we knew what was at stake with our life, I believe we would trust God a little bit more. Jesus has given us a reminder through what He tells Peter. The enemy wants to ruin you, and we have to be ready. I am an avid boxing fan and some of the worst mistakes happen when a fighter has knocked his opponent down and thinks

---

11 *The New King James Version.* (1982). (1 Sa 17:9). Nashville: Thomas Nelson.

that the match is over. A knockdown is celebratory but remain focused because your opponent might not be down for the count. David understand this, *"51 Therefore David ran and stood over the Philistine, took his sword and drew it out of its sheath and killed him, and cut off his head with it."*[12] David made sure that Goliath was dead, similarly to our giants in life we have to cut the head off of our challengers otherwise, they may get up to inflict the same pain that we attempted to inflict on them. David did not let Goliath hang around, taking out the giant is a part of the process. This was their champion; this was their leader and David destroyed that. Upon his annihilation of Goliath, the Philistines fled and the newfound confidence of the Israelite army because their champion had been defeated. This defeat began before David took aim with his slingshot. This defeat began when David proclaims his faith in the Lord. Your victory begins with your priorities, and David knew as a man of God, where his faith and focus should be. We cannot expect to be victorious consistently over our giants if we refrain from focusing on the foundation of our strength.

2*The Lord is my strength and song,*
And He has become my salvation;

---

12 *The New King James Version.* (1982). (1 Sa 17:51). Nashville: Thomas Nelson.

He is my God, and I will praise Him;
My father's God, and I will exalt Him.
3The Lord is a man of war;
The Lord is His name.[13]

Exodus 15:2–3 (NKJV)

---

13 *The New King James Version.* (1982). (Ex 15:2–3). Nashville: Thomas Nelson.

A Giant Stands in the Way of Your Appointment

In history, some of our greatest leaders took on some giants. Medgar Evers who was a part of the desegregation of Ole Miss took down a giant. Dr. Martin Luther King took on racism, oppression, economic segregation, and those are giants we are still fighting today. Angela Davis and many others like Michelle Alexander aim to bring awareness to things like mass incarceration. These things are giants, and these things stand in the way of your appointment. Every obstacle allows us access to our appointment. David was chosen by God but understand that even though he was chosen by God, he still had tasks to complete. David did not do this because king was on the horizon, he did this because he loved his people. It is the proverbial cherry on top when a lover of the people ends up leading the people.

Then David spoke to the men who stood by him, saying, "What shall be done for the man who kills this Philistine and takes away the reproach from Israel? For whom is this uncircumcised Philistine, that he should defy the armies of the living God?"[14]

1 Samuel 17:26 (NKJV)

Your appointment is an identifier. It is a part of the plan that David become king, but prior to the implementation of any appointment there may be some major things we have to overcome. Understand David's mindset is one that we ought to have no matter the situation. He saw Goliath through the eyes of being protected by God, no matter the circumstance. Who is this Philistine that he should disrespect the armies of the living God? It's imperative that we approach life's situations with this mindset. When your expectation is God centered and you have faith that the outcome will be what is best for you, you do not have to worry.

What we must expect, is the fact that just as much as we see our giant, so do the people around us. Typically, we have talked about this problem, we have asked prayer for this problem, and maybe even sought advice on this problem. Therefore, people know the giant in our life. Goliath poses an interesting dynamic to the life

---

14 *The New King James Version.* (1982). (1 Sa 17:26). Nashville: Thomas Nelson.

of David. David is not a soldier in the army, but a loss by the Israelite army to the Philistines would directly impact his sense of freedom. Giants can pose a sense of fear, and then we find ourselves beginning to rationalize life after failure. David does not do that even after his brother provides discouragement in David's direction.

Now Eliab his oldest brother heard when he spoke to the men; and Eliab's anger was aroused against David, and he said, "Why did you come down here? And with whom have you left those few sheep in the wilderness? I know your pride and the insolence of your heart, for you have come down to see the battle."[15]

1 Samuel 17:28 (NKJV)

No one knows us like family, right? Was there some truth to the statement that Eliab made? The characteristics of insolence and pride are definitely shown in the character of David as progress with the story of his life, but in this moment David was there out of obedience to his father and decided to speak his mind in the midst of his people hanging in the balance of bondage and freedom.

---

15 *The New King James Version.* (1982). (1 Sa 17:28). Nashville: Thomas Nelson.

*And David said, "What have I done now? Is there not a
cause?" 30 Then he turned from him toward another and said
the same thing; and these people answered him as the first
ones did.*[16]

1 Samuel 17:29–30 (NKJV)

David understood his why; David understood his
faith in God. "Is there not a cause?" You may have to
ask yourself that question while you are staring at the
giants in your life right now. If your appointment has
purpose next to it, then your giant needs to fall, and you
need to take the giant out. In this moment what are you
waiting for? What is holding you up from letting that
slingshot fly? Remember even family will be perplexed
as your motivation to respond with is there not a cause.
Do not let that discourage you, do not let that distract
you from the fact that Goliath has been taunting your
people for the past forty days and if no one does anything about it, it could have a bondage type of effect on
a high number of people. In this case an entire nation!

---

16 *The New King James Version.* (1982). (1 Sa 17:29–30). Nashville:
Thomas Nelson.

Goliath is Not the Finish Line

Throughout my entire life I have heard Romans 8:28 used as a tool of encouragement. This text is often used when things are not going our way, or we are going through a tough time. I also liken this text to a race. Imagine you run a race, you win the race, and no one presents you with a medal or a trophy. What if I told you that just running that race was a part of God's plan? Defeating your giants is not the finish line. It is a great accomplishment and do not forget to celebrate even the smallest accomplishments because it is a blessing to accomplish anything you put your mind to. Many times, we see the other side of an accomplishment as a time to rest, but I suggest that you feed off that momentum and really put your mind to preparing yourself for the next obstacle. In a sport like football getting a first down after a 3rd and long with the game on the line, is a very difficult task but you still need a touchdown or field goal to win the game. I may celebrate for a moment, but I have to line back up and stay focused because we have a game to win. God has king goals for David, defeating Goliath was just a big third down conversion on the game winning drive.

And we know that all things work together for good to those who love God, to those who are the called according to His purpose.[17]

Romans 8:28 (NKJV)

Most manuscripts, both early and late, have "all things work together," but a few manuscripts have, "God works all things together." The difference is the inclusion of God as the subject, instead of "all things."[18] There is a gigantic difference in viewpoint or paradigm when we look at it from a God works all things perspective. When I look at all my issues, obstacles, and goals with a God is working all of these things together for my benefit, I then realize how to compartmentalize what is in front of me. The initial challenge from Goliath was not so David would be a hero, he saw the plight of his people hanging in the balance.

---

17 *The New King James Version.* (1982). (Ro 8:28). Nashville: Thomas Nelson.
18 Brannan, R., & Loken, I. (2014). *The Lexham Textual Notes on the Bible* (Ro 8:28). Bellingham, WA: Lexham Press.

I have done a number of things in the community, most recently we have had the ability to pressure political officials for a grant to begin a program to make the area of Linden a lot safer. Getting the initial grant is a victory but it is not the end result. We are still faced with the giant of young people of color being murdered in the communities they live. We are still faced with comforting the grandmother who is raising her grandchildren because her child is dead, incarcerated, or has neglected her children. This grandmother who wants to send her children to the park to play cannot because it is just not safe. These are community Goliaths and we need a David that is going to stand toe to toe with the giant and say No more. My mother is a single mother, and her giant was raising four boys by herself, and in effort to defeat the giant she took the Hannah approach. She prayed specifically that God take care of us in her absence. She was a nurse and she worked part time doing home health contracts and refereeing high school and college sports. There were many evenings that she was not home so that we would have food, lights, and clothes. She stood in the face of the giant of a broken family and dedicated her sons to God just had he had given us to her. There were plenty of tears, struggles and frustrations but she knew the plight that hung in the balance if she did not do what God had asked her to do. This was not just a giant faced by her but a giant that plagues the black community. One in four children in the United States are raised by a single parent. Of that 25 percent, 72 percent of those children are black children.

Nonetheless, thank God for the parents that looked that proverbial Goliath in the eye and said, "Is there not a cause?" I know it is gut wrenching raising children on your own, but there is a cause. God is working all things together! Those children you are raising while staring a bank account that does not have enough money to provide groceries until the next payday. God has a king and queen calling on their life and He expects you to be a part of pulling that out of them, even when things seem impossible. When you look at your child you see a smart son or daughter, you see a child emotionally fragile due to the woes of a broken family but God sees a king in their future, a queen in their future. I am often reminded of Ruth, I imagine during the death of her father-in-law, brother-in-law, and husband while experiencing famine, the idea of a Boaz seemed far-fetched, but had she not aligned herself with Naomi during this time of need, the story ends a lot earlier than it should. The return to Judah was celebratory, they were now in a place in which they could at least eat and have shelter and that is a blessing. Even during the return to Judah there was a focus that was needed to know that this is not the finish line. God had Matthew chapter 1 plans way back in Ruth and it is up to us to understand there is a bigger legacy that is to be left that is greater than the first down you just completed.

This is the beauty of finding joy in all situations. "Sometimes we become so focused on the finish line, that we fail to find joy in the journey." The finish line is a goal that is a part of the journey but do not become so hyper focused on the journey that you do not find joy in every accomplishment or blessing along the way. Imagine if David would have bowed out gracefully after defeating Goliath. We would have no king, there would be no Solomon, his name would not be mentioned in the lineage of Jesus. It is almost like the high school sports phenom that is still gloating about the state championship that happened twenty years ago at the current high school and has done nothing since. People probably still revere the athlete; they probably have a love for the nostalgia, but eventually that memory is only going to get you so far. I know plenty of teammates that I had during high school that have did nothing with the talent that God gave them after their athletic ability had run its course. I had plenty of successes during my first ministry, and plenty of Goliaths that I had to stand in the face of. If I get to a place of stagnation and think that the rehashing of successes in the face of the parishioners will sustain their peace of progress, I am sadly mistaken. Yes, David killed Goliath, yes David avoided death at the hands of Saul, but there were still citizens of his country and his family that needed shepherding even after those accomplishments.

Sometimes the biggest giants we face are the beginning to success. This is the first step of reference that prepares us for a long list of accomplishments during his reign as king. David states in the 34th Psalm, *I sought the Lord, and He heard me, and delivered me from all my fears.*[19] David understood that as long as he was living, God's purpose was to be walked in. We must know that God is a deliverer, sometimes it takes a moment of uncertainty to know what God can do. As confident of David was, many of the people around him believed he was signing his death certificate fighting this giant who had been a champion since his youth. To find joy in the worst circumstance we must know who the deliverer of our fears is. We must prioritize seeking God and understanding that even fear, failure, and success are a part of the plan because he is working all things together for us. The determining factor in how it works out for us depends on our ability to serve the Lord.

---

19 *The New King James Version.* (1982). (Ps 34:4). Nashville: Thomas Nelson.

Leading After the Mistakes

Some of the worst mistakes I have made happened when I was not where I was supposed to be in a given time. I remember in middle school, I consistently walked home. My mother knew my route, and typically that was the way she drove home and if she got off work early enough to meet me along my route she would stop and I would get in the car. Somedays, I thought I was smart, I figured, *well it was 4:00 p.m. and it took me thirty minutes to get home*, I might stop at a friend's house. They would tell me, "Do not worry about it, my parents will take you home." Typically, my mother assumed I would be home around 4:30-4:45 p.m.. One of my cousins worked at the Dollar General on the way home and I would go in and buy a cold drink especially as it got closer to summer because that Texas heat is nothing to play with, so that was my grace period. It was always interesting that the days a friend said their parents would bring me home were days their parents would get home late, typically I knew my mom would call the house phone around 4:45 p.m., so if I was at my friend's house and not home, I would call her and typically cover up my story to buy myself a little bit of time. The consequence was when I had to walk home from a friend's house that lived further from my house than the school was, my mom would make me walk home. When we go out of our way to cover up things or go out of our way to be in places that we should not be, the walk back home is always longer than it was intended to be.

David had an episode in his primetime drama series in which he was not where he was supposed to be. As leaders, we must be careful when our team has risen to a place in which they no longer need their leader to win on the battlefield. Often, when we get to a place of success, we have two options. We can continue to develop people, or we can relax and think everything is okay and we have time to RELAX. Relaxation is necessary and everyone needs some time off. Nonetheless, when relaxation leads to the absence of responsibility, we set ourselves up for failure or ending up in a place where we should never be in the first place. Imagine if David had been at battle, imagine if David was even focused on hearing back from his men and not in an idle place of nothing to do.

It happened in the spring of the year, at the time when kings go out to battle, that David sent Joab and his servants with him, and all Israel; and they destroyed the people of Ammon and besieged Rabbah. But David remained at Jerusalem.[20]

2 Samuel 11:1 (NKJV)

We must be careful when surroundings are comfortable. It is the spring, the weather is nice, David has taken this sabbatical and he is back at the camp. He is probably in a good mood, his army has just won, and won big. They destroyed and besieged the opponent, and instead of David being there to celebrate with his men, he is alone, with no accountability and David's temptation gets the best of David's self-control. Satan has a particularly good way at setting things up to be distraction free when he wants to attack you in the way that will destroy you for the long haul. Thankfully, God is a forgiving God but let's take a look at the situation.

Then it happened one evening that David arose from his bed and walked on the roof of the king's house. And from the roof he saw a woman bathing, and the woman was very beautiful to behold.[21]

2 Samuel 11:2 (NKJV)

20 *The New King James Version.* (1982). (2 Sa 11:1). Nashville: Thomas Nelson.
21 *The New King James Version.* (1982). (2 Sa 11:2). Nashville: Thomas Nelson.

One of the most dangerous things in life is to see something that is off limits in a realm that you should not be viewing them in. We always must consider our vantage point. Understand David was on the roof, Bathsheba was not. It is not too far-fetched to say that the majority of people probably walked on the ground and could not see what Bathsheba was doing. David could, and when we end up seeing things that we should not see, we have a decision to make: do we investigate or do we walk away? Investigation is the toughest part, but often times if we refrain from investigating, we avoid slipping.

Historically speaking, Bathsheba was performing her monthly purification rites. In this period of vulnerability as a leader we have to know better than to make decisions as such. It's safe to say that David's influence, David's reach, led to him to take advantage of Bathsheba. The Bible states that she was purifying herself from her monthly uncleanness according to 2 Samuel 11:4. David did not just interrupt a normal afternoon bath; he interrupted a ritual of purification. Bathsheba was not the enticer, but David took advantage of a vulnerable time. Her husband was off to war, David is a man of influence. Not only did David commit adultery, adultery was punishable by death and Bathsheba's life was at stake.

As a leader, we should not put the people that depend on us in harm's way due to our lack of responsibility. We typically talk about the fact that David slept with a married woman, or that David had Bathsheba's husband killed, nonetheless in that moment he also put Bathsheba's life in jeopardy. We must know, as a leader, the choices we make affect more than just us. As a father, my decisions affect my wife, my children, and can have generational effects on my family. We have to be completely honest about the fact that this is a traumatic situation and when we believe we can cover-up trauma, we typically add more trauma to an already traumatic situation. It is imperative that our mistakes are the outpour of unchecked desires. David sent his messengers, and they took Bathsheba. David is King, he has influence, he has a following and he makes orders, yet he uses his influence for the wrong purpose. After we make a mistake, we have a choice to make. We can be accountable for the mistake and own up to it, or we can continue to cover it up until it unravels right in your lap. When you are going through rough times you need a Nathan. You need someone who can hold you accountable yet encourage you to walk in your purpose. One thing that grace and mercy shows us is that one mistake does not negate everything that God has done on your behalf. David was chosen by God; therefore, man could not take what they did not assign. David was delivered from the hand of Saul, David had a home, wives, and many resources yet what he had was not enough. This is the defining factor of leadership, is contentment a characteristic of your leadership?

Women are not going anywhere. No matter how old we become, how much success we attain or accolades we earn, if not women, there will always be a temptation that you will have to ask God to protect you from yourself. Dear leader, you have to be wise and transparent with yourself and know what you can and cannot handle. It is alright to admit something to God and to yourself and ask for his protection, every game has a mismatch, and the enemy understands how to exploit every issue we have. This is why we need God, without Him we are no match for the temptation at hand. Furthermore, leading after a mistake becomes impossible without the grace and mercy of God.

Understand that consequences do not mean that grace and mercy do not exist.

"The Lord also has put away your sin; you shall not die. 14 However, because by this deed you have given great occasion to the enemies of the Lord to blaspheme, the child also who is born to you shall surely die. "[22]

2 Samuel 12:13–14 (NKJV)

---

22 *The New King James Version.* (1982). (2 Sa 12:13–14). Nashville: Thomas Nelson.

David still had a daunting consequence, but if we take into consideration what David did to get to this place, it does not seem like cruel and unusual punishment, nonetheless throughout all of this, God is still by his side. Remember as a leader, God is always by your side no matter how dark things become. Sometimes grace is allowing you to stay in your position and lead through a storm rather than removal being the consequence of choice.

Messing up is not fun. Sometimes a mess up results in job loss, problems with families, a past that people never allow you to live down. Many people ask the question or will ask the question, "Can God still use me?" As men in the church, we limit use to position when God never intended for it to be that way. Designation does not merit effectiveness. On the same note, your past does not decide whether God will use you in His Kingdom or not. We serve a God that has used some people from all walks of life, income levels, and races in effort to save his people, spread his gospel, and teach his word to individuals all across the world.

Moses was born during a period when social injustices to the Israelites was alive and well. To the point that the king at that time was killing young baby boys to control the ability to oppress Hebrew people. Nonetheless, the faith of his mother placed him in the hands of Pharaoh's daughter, provided a great education for him, and a prosperous future in Egypt, if he so desired. Many of us despite the neighborhoods we grew up in, the single parent homes we lived in, the hardworking father that we had does not nullify the fact that many of us have made mistakes that are completely contrary to the way we were raised.

I know as you read this book, there are probably mistakes that you remember right now. That mistake is not the end, there might be a detour but nonetheless God does not make mistakes. You might not be leading a country, a Fortune 500 company, or leading a church, but that does not mean that you cannot have impact after a mistake. There are times in which your mistake will allow you to have a greater impact on the community, city, and the world.

The Importance of Fidelity and Loyalty

There are a bunch of characteristics that a leader must have. A couple of them that make you dependable is the ability to be loyal and to operate with a high level of fidelity. Be mindful that I did not say perfection, but loyalty and fidelity. It is very interesting how fidelity works; we typically associate it with the term infidelity which has destroyed marriages. Nonetheless, the unfaithfulness does not begin with the act but typically something nestled deep within the roots of our make-up that causes us to make unwise decisions. One of the things I learned in therapy, yes, your preacher went to therapy- as leaders we cannot afford to fall victim to the vulnerabilities that arise due to a lack of assertive communication about what we need. I honestly advise it to every leader, regardless of your capacity of leadership.

If you are a coach, senior manager for a banking organization, store leader at your local grocery chain or a preacher you need to talk to someone. I cannot be the husband I need to be if I do not allow my wife inside to what is going through my mind. I cannot become a prisoner of my own mind, because eventually that leads to frustration and resentment.

Fidelity is deeper than not making mistakes, because we all will make mistakes one way or another. Fidelity is being accountable for your actions because you are loyal. Officially defined as faithfulness to a person, cause, or belief, demonstrated by continuing loyalty and support. Fidelity happens from a place of demonstration; demonstrating your loyalty, demonstrating your love, demonstrating the ability to work hard. Jesus demonstrated His faithfulness to us by devoting His entire life to being a place of refuge for us. Each place in which you get to exercise your ability to be a leader, you should treat it like it might be your last, you never know what impact you can have on people just by being honest and working hard. You might not have all the resources, you might not have the unlimited budget but there is nothing that should get in the way of you working hard and being loyal to the people that God allows you lead. Be mindful every pasture does not need you to shepherd it forever, you might be preparing the sheep for another shepherd, but as my grandma says,

"You need to leave it better than you found it." There will times in which you want to give up because loyalty does not always beget support.

Preparing the Next Generation for God's 'Yes' after God tells Your Generation 'No' (Solomon Builds the Temple)

But God said to me, 'You shall not build a house for My name, because you have been a man of war and have shed blood.' 4 However the Lord God of Israel chose me above all the house of my father to be king over Israel forever, for He has chosen Judah to be the ruler. And of the house of Judah, the house of my father, and among the sons of my father, He was pleased with me to make me king over all Israel.[23]

1 Chronicles 28:3–4 (NKJV)

5 Now David said, "Solomon my son is young and inexperienced, and the house to be built for the Lord must be exceedingly magnificent, famous and glorious throughout all countries. I will now make preparation for it." So, David made abundant preparations before his death.

6 Then he called for his son Solomon and charged him to build a house for the Lord God of Israel. 7 And David said to Solomon: "My son, as for me, it was in my mind to build a

---

23 *The New King James Version.* (1982). (1 Ch 28:3–4). Nashville: Thomas Nelson.

house to the name of the Lord my God; 8 but the word of the Lord came to me, saying, 'You have shed much blood and have made great wars; you shall not build a house for My name, because you have shed much blood on the earth in My sight. 9 Behold, a son shall be born to you, who shall be a man of rest; and I will give him rest from all his enemies all around.[24]

1 Chronicles 22:5–9 (NKJV)

There is a portion of leadership that I believe is one of the most important parts of leadership and that is legacy. We speak often about leaving a financial legacy for our loved ones and even our churches but there is another legacy that is just as important. That is the legacy of faith, that is the legacy service, that is the legacy of leadership. Leaders in our churches do not just arrive, someone must raise them up. If you have children, your faith, and your competencies such as leadership, honesty, and integrity should be passed down just like properties, heirlooms, and money. There was an exact reason that God would not allow David to build the house of God, there were many instances of spilled blood, there were instances of trauma within the family of David, and although God did not allow David to build a temple, God did not rob David of preparing Solomon for this legacy driven task. It is imperative that we lead

---

24 *The New King James Version.* (1982). (1 Ch 22:5–9). Nashville: Thomas Nelson.

within the confines that God has placed us. Do not be attracted to the will that others have on your life, you must be in tune with the vision that God has placed on your life. Did God allow David to build the temple? No, but that did not stop him from being a king to the people of God, or a father to Solomon. One of the worst mistakes we can make is not teaching those running behind us how to carry the torch someone lit for us.

David understood that there would be kings before him and after him. Fortunately, the king after him was his son. We also have to be prepared that our children may not be in the same realm of leadership that we are in. One of my very close friends is the son of a very prominent minister within the churches of Christ. I have typically leaned on him for advice as it pertains to his paradigm of being a preacher's son. One of the things that has stuck with me over the countless conversations that we have had is that his father never prohibited him from exercising the gifts and talents that God bestowed on him. He is not a preacher, but he is an excellent teacher of God's word, he even leads a weekly young adult Bible study, he's a song leader, he's currently working on his PhD, married and teaching at Florida A&M University. It does not take an expert to know that someone raised him right. Someone prepared him for a life of service, discipleship, and discipline.

Adulthood is a daunting task, and someone must prepare us for it. We have dreams and aspirations and could have the talent to achieve those dreams. Nonetheless, if no one prepares us for the task at hand, failure can be on the horizon. David acknowledges where his son lacks experience and suggest that preparation must take place. Although this was in the mind of David, he did not feel slighted because God told him 'no.' Instead, he put all that energy in preparing Solomon for the task at hand. One of the things young leaders need are mentors, a new position is essentially like drinking from the fire hose but if there is someone there to help us along the way it can make a world of difference. Watch what God did when David agreed to prepare Solomon, he brought peace to the land. Transition is peaceful when preparation is prioritized during the process. I have had the pleasure of being in leadership roles at a few congregations and the healthiest situations were always due to the leader before me paving the way. I remember when Rudolph Johnson stood before Roeser Road church and endorsed my abilities to lead that church through transition. He blessed me abundantly, I remember sitting at his house for hours upon end and talking about ministry. He taught me some fundamental principles that I use to this day. He explained to me the things he wished he had done better and the things he did well. He honestly is the reason

I try to be as thorough as possible with application and illustrations in my sermons. That came because of what he gave me.

I remember sitting at the house of a man that had one of the most extensive libraries I had ever seen, and he told me, "Hey, I'm done. You can have all of these books and my manuscripts." It was like a goldmine, over forty years of sermon preparation and scholarship. Some of those books I still have, many of those sermons I digitized and studied like I was preparing for the bar exam, it literally changed my ministry forever. I'm reminded of Jesse Fogle, whom I truly refer to as my father in the gospel, he gave me an opportunity to preach when I had no experience and could barely exegete the text. I had the ability to start my own state youth conference because of men like Deacon Wyrick, Fate Hagood, and Kevin Murray.

There is also another factor that leads into preparing for a new leader and that is preparing the people for the new leader that is about to step into the position. The people probably saw Solomon grow up, the people probably knew things about Solomon's childhood that he could not remember, but that is not enough to garner the respect when you move from child to leader of people. People have to be taught how to embrace transition; I have seen many assignments end horribly because no one was taught how to embrace change.

Then David said, "This is the house of the Lord God, and this is the altar of burnt offering for Israel." 2 So David commanded to gather the aliens who were in the land of Israel; and he appointed masons to cut hewn stones to build the house of God.[25]

1 Chronicles 22:1–2 (NKJV)

Not only did David prepare those who belonged to the house of God, David prepared the community. This is a press release that would affect the entire land. Similar to presidential endorsements, they are important. It is necessary for a leader to vouch for who is up next, when the leader does not vouch for the next man or woman up it is difficult for the people to embrace them. It is a difficult task to win the hearts and minds of people even when transition is done the right way, but when it is not done at all people only have their experience depend on. When this happens, people spend their entire assignment being measured up to the predecessor rather than held accountable to the oracles of God, who is responsible for the leader in the first place. Support looks different when transition is done in a healthy way. Upon moving to Ohio, I knew I would be working with men and women that I had never worked with before. People I did not know and

---

25 *The New King James Version.* (1982). (1 Ch 22:1–2). Nashville: Thomas Nelson.

would have to get to know, but when people trust the decision and have been taught to embrace transition, work becomes more effective and efficient. Imagine if Saul had prepared David rather than trying to preserve what was left of his kingship. David had to depend on foreign nations, deal with a divided kingdom, and run for his life because of faulty leadership. Churches have died because people fail to implement healthy transition plans. It is fearful to let go but it is dangerous to hold on too long. We know that God did not give us the spirit of fear, we must have faith that the decisions we make will be carried out properly due to the foresight of God. It may not be in the church, it may not be in your home, but spirituality, faith and adulthood must be taught because no one holds on to a position forever.

The Balance Between Bully and Push-Over

Being Christlike Does not Mean Being a Coward: The Balance Between Bully and Push-Over

In the fifth grade I was picked on horrendously. I was overweight, I had crooked teeth and because of my size I typically had to shop in the grown men's section. That meant I dressed like my older cousins in the mid-nineties instead of like a ten-year-old kid. When I tell you I got picked on it I am probably not giving you enough information. It was horrible, but I have to thank my mom because the way she complimented me and my brothers, we did not pay much attention to the insults and the criticisms of other people in school.

At the beginning of the fifth grade it was easier for my brother Quincy and I to attend the school where my mother worked. This school was probably in the worst part of town with kids that lived lives that we had no idea about. I remember one kid used to pick on me and my mother being the school nurse ended up having to do a home visit at this student's house. At the time, I thought it was just a goodwill visit until my mother would not let me come in the house with her, I had to sit on the porch with my brother and wait for her to get done with her visit. Looking back, I believe my mother saw something at the school being a nurse which prompted her to visit the child's home. I'll never forget as my mom opened the door; I saw what I thought was a couch but happened to be just a bench with an old sheet on it. It taught me a lesson, although I was getting picked on these students that lived in the apartment complex across from the school had a much worse home experience than I had. They dealt with transient housing, drug use from older family members, and in all reality an impoverished lifestyle that I knew nothing about.

We were by no means rich or well off, but we did okay when my parents were married. My father was a police officer and my mother was a nurse. I remember the ride home my mother explained to me that some kids were jealous of what they assumed my life was like. Even seeing the reality of their life did not help the bullying, eventually I ended up having to fight a few times. Even though I grew up in suburbs, my grandmother's house was in one of the roughest neighborhoods in Dallas, Texas. I spent a lot of time there, had some of my first fights on that block, so fear was not one of my character traits. I got in plenty of fights, I was stabbed in the classroom in the fifth grade and fought on a number of occasions. So much so, that my mother ended up transferring me to the school by my house for safety reasons. It was safer to allow me to walk home than to keep me in a school in which I had to fight every week. Here is where the issued lied, once people began to come to the realization I could fight a certain confidence attached to that notoriety and I abused it in some instances because instead of walking away I engaged in fighting because of the reputation that came with being a kid in that school who had "hands".

In order to lay the foundation, you have to find balance, anyone who is laying foundation before they pour the concrete they have to make sure where they are laying a foundation, it must be balanced.

Structure is everything. If your church doubled in size tomorrow do you have the structure to handle it? I know it sounds farfetched, but our foundation needs to reflect our vision. The tough part about navigation is finding balance for the old folks who reminisce on the old way.

How do we pay homage to the history that is resented by the new generation that views the history through the lens of ignorance and oppression? One of the things a mentor shared with me was, "Remember one day, young preachers, we will be the seventy-year-old men remembering yester-year." In order to navigate the re-build, you have to find balance between the praise and the pain. Even when there is something to praise God about, there some comfort that people need about the pain they are going through. Even when everyone is go-ing through pain, there is still something to praise God about. God deserves the praise at the small victories as well as the completed triumphs. Do not defraud God of praise because all you laid was the foundation. You might not be able to erect a building but thank God that you are a part of the foundation laying. Why should foundation laying inspire praise? Understand who the foundation builders are.

In leadership there, is a balance that must be had. Even if your disposition is intimidating, you never want to lead from a place of fear. Leading from a place of ser-vice is always a better alternative that provides comfort to those that follow you. If you are leading from a place of fear, eventually that leads to resentment for many of the people who are depending on you for leadership.

One thing we have to do is reflect, if we are the bully, we need to look at why we have these traits. Is it because we were bullied or betrayed? Therefore, we attempt to preserve our dignity or fearlessness by attempting to put up these walls of strength because we feel like everyone is always out to get us. I know this mentality even caused me to refrain from building relationships with older men who could have been great mentors. I did not trust older men in ministry, not because I did not want a proverbial Jethro, but because I felt neglected by my father. Surprisingly, I saw relationships with other older men through the lens of neglect from my father. I truly became the epitome of the song by J. Cole entitled "No More Role Modelz." I figured if I had made it this far on my own, I did not need help from anyone older than me I could figure it out on my own, and if anyone wanted to help I saw it as an attack on my skill set and I put up walls and shut people out.

Typically, I would intentionally act unapproachable because I felt the need to continuously protect myself. This affected me to a point in which I would even minister from this place of self-preservation. There was one minister who approached me in a manner to help me and ended up betraying me due to a sense of ignorance and my true need for assistance being young in ministry. I have found that trusting people is a part of the job description but just because one person betrays you does not mean that you must shut everyone out. Imagine if David would have treated every older man like he did Saul, he would have never been able to seek rest or delegate properly for help. In ministry, you are going to meet some Sauls along the way, but you will also be blessed with some Nathans. A Nathan is going to hold you accountable, but Nathan is not going to want anything from you but to see you want in your purpose. Nathan told David, "You are the man." Understand that Nathan and Jonathan make dealing with Saul a lot easier. That way when you find yourself in the dark cave of life with the ability to expose Saul and destroy him or everything he is worth, you will walk away dignified showing him the hem of his garment you cut off, acknowledging the fact that through all the darts you threw at my head, the extra steps Saul takes to keep you from your appointment will never measure up to the anointing that God has provided on your life.

Leading Your Family Through Trauma

When I read this story, I thought about our Black Women. I thought about how I was raised by a Black Woman who worked as a nurse during the day, refereed basketball, and made sure that the needs of four boys were met. Meanwhile, she never missed a football game, parent teacher conference, or a track meet. I've thought about the amount of oppression, ridicule, and cultural misappropriation that women of color experience on the job, in our homes and in our churches. In the midst of the outpour of the hashtag #metoo movement, initiated by Tarana Burke, a black woman and things in pop culture in particular surviving R. Kelly. I believe that as Men of God we need to be a protector of our women and not a contributor to their oppression and abuse.

We are cognizant of David's experience with Bathsheba, the sin of having sex with someone else's wife. Having her husband killed meanwhile impregnating Bathsheba. This cycle of sin spilled over to his children in which the Bible says, "Now therefore, the sword shall never depart from your house, because you have despised Me and have taken the wife of Uriah the Hittite to be your wife." Here we have Amnon and Tamar, in this story Amnon forces himself on his own sister. We may look at this story with the eye of "that would never happen in my family." This text brings to life the fact that ninety percent of victims know their abuser. Historically, our women have been abused as early as this text, to years of abuse on plantations, to exploitation in music, film, and social media and it is time we protect our women.

Currently, I am finishing up a Trauma Informed Care Certification Program right here in the state of Ohio. Being in my leadership role I have had firsthand knowledge of some of the trauma that happens in our churches. I had an interview on my podcast *Community Conversations* in which the young lady, Amber Baldwin of *Sunflower Power* podcast unapologetically stated, "The church cannot heal something it is responsible for." I honestly was floored, because every Sunday across this world you can find a church with a message of hope somewhere. What does that message of hope sound like in a place where you are not heard or your voice is suppressed, when I do not have the ability to speak up, the shame begins to eat away at me and eventually I can even believe that it is my fault. I remember watching a study on trauma in which the researcher put these mice in a cage and would provide electric shock to the feet of the mice. Eventually the electric shock was so traumatizing that when he opened the cage they did not want to leave.

Sometimes we subject ourselves to bottling trauma because we have never been able to talk about it. I become a prisoner to my own thoughts when my life is absent from empathy and support no matter what I have been through. I believe that some of us have not considered the factors of embarrassment that are packaged with being a victim. The young man or lady that is now hopeful from a sermon as they deal with the aftermath of abuse, but wants to come to the altar of healing but does not want to express the pain that they went through. Or the woman who is being physically abused by her husband and everyone in the church knows but the trauma experienced has not given her the courage to walk away, and the abuser happens to be an active ministry leader. What we have to realize that talking about the victim behind their back or giving them glaring looks as they self-consciously walk to their seat on the pew because Sunday service is the only hope they experience.

My predecessor told me as the pastor I have to be comfortable with taking out the trash, and dealing with abuse is the trash that has to be taken out of our pews, out of our classrooms, and out of our culture. Sweeping these issues under the rug is a practice that we need to retire. We cannot deny the inevitable that abuse has happened in our places of worship, in our homes and in our neighborhoods. I doubt this was something that Tamar, David's daughter expected to happen to her. It's one thing for our parishioners to experience abuse but it is a totally different sense of defeat for the victim when we fail to handle it accordingly. Essentially, we have allowed our churches to become places of pain and triggers of past trauma rather than centers of hope and a place where everyone feels like family.

The University of Baylor in Waco, Texas did a study on clergy sexual misconduct:

- More than 3% of women who had attended a congregation in the past month reported that they had been the object of CSM at some time in their adult lives;
- 92% of these sexual advances had been made in secret, not in open dating relationships; and
- 67% of the offenders were married to someone else at the time of the advance.

- In the average American congregation of 400 persons, with women representing, on average, 60% of the congregation, there are, on average, of 7 women who have experienced clergy sexual misconduct.
- Of the entire sample, 8% report having known about CSM occurring in a congregation they have attended. Therefore, in the average American congregation of 400 congregants, there are, on average, 32 persons who have experienced CSM in their community of faith.

These are glaring statistics that have ruined church families, split congregations, and traumatized families. When things like this happen, it destroys the fabric of what God created church to be. Many of these families and the congregation itself, is typically never the same. One choice that has to be made by the leader of the family is a choice of protection, a choice to seek justice, and a choice to hold people accountable. When we attempt to keep secrets for the sake of images, we end up doing more damage to our own family. We have to stand up for our children as leaders, especially when it comes to the trauma of our children. There is a story of David's daughter Tamar who was raped by her own brother and the Bible explains that once her older brother Absalom found out he told his sister to keep quiet about it, and we also see that David was angry about the situation he did not hold his son accountable like he should have. Our society has even positioned itself to not hold many of our abusers accountable for the deeds that they have done because of status, affluence, or public stature. For every Amnon that we protect there is a Tamar that is scarred for life because we failed to defend her, we failed to respond to her trauma, in turn we have abused individuals in the church that leave because of embarrassment and lack of protection.

Listen, as leaders of our household if we do not defend our family no one else will. If we do not deal with the trauma under our roof, it will have a way of dealing with us. As you move through 1 Samuel you see that this is something that David has not dealt with, meanwhile the brother that is angry about how his sister was raped has been plotting, during this plan he ends up killing his brother. This possibly could have been avoided had David dealt with this issue in a manner that protected the needs of Tamar. David did get angry as the text tells us, but emotions do not fix issues. Trauma response is more than just showing an emotion of disproval. In our households, in our churches, how are we making space for the abused, the neglected, the people who have been hurt by the church. Grace makes space for everyone, no one should ever feel embarrassed about bringing their problems to Jesus. David's failure to respond to the trauma that his daughter experienced not only caused his daughter to live with a horrendous experience, but also the loss of a son. Let us not lose our family due to the failure to respond effectively to the issues that traumatize our family.

It was customary that the older brother would be the caretaker of his sisters. This is why she seeks comfort from her brother Absalom. The issue is that the cycle does not stop it is just enhanced because instead of Absalom seeking God to be his avenger, he takes matters into his own hands and kills his brother. Do not sweep the dirt of family history under the rug, it does nothing but leave room for rugs to be pulled up and cycles to continue to be reinforced. We have to end cycles of abuse, neglect, hurt and dysfunction. God desires that there be peace in our families, not hidden cycles of deceit and abuse. We have to stop victim shaming; we must protect our young girls and our young women! Everyone is this room might not have a daughter to protect, but you have a sister, a niece, a mother, a grandmother, a auntie, a co-worker! There is someone you can protect!

We can have the best small groups, worship with high energy and legendary preaching but the failure to respond to the problems of people that make up the church can damage our families and the credibility of the church for generations.

Even if a child or adult hints that abuse has occurred, as leaders, we should encourage him or her to talk freely by avoiding all judgmental comments. According to the American Academy of Child and Adolescent Psychiatry, it imperative that we should show that we are taking the person seriously, studies show that people who are listened to an understood share more and have less problems emotionally than a person who has been completely dismissed or portrayed as telling an untruth. Healing comes from understanding and listening. It is very important that we assure the person that they have done the right thing by telling what is happening, the child or adult could feel frightened because many abusers will threaten the person by telling them that they will harm people in their circle if they were to tell.

Remove all blame from the victim, most victims will attempt to make sense out of the abuse and think they may have even caused it or that the abuse is some sort of punishment for the wrongdoings they have committed in their life. One of the most important things we must do as leaders or parents, is offer protection, helping the person to understand that we will do whatever it takes to ensure they are protected. If we take these steps, we have a better chance at changing a culture that has caused many people to not feel safe inside a place of refuge like a church or a ministry team.

Your Baggage is Delaying Your Mission

I will admit that I am a light packer. When I go to the airport, I check everything I possibly can. When I am walking to my gate the most I want on my person is a backpack. My wife typically has to pretty much force me to take my iPad and my Laptop because I try my best to leave one of them at home if the work that needs to be accomplished can happen on one or the other device. In my backpack is usually my toiletry bag, my electronics, a charger, a bottle of water and typically a snack. My snack of choice is typically anything spicy or trial mix of some sort. My middle name should be personal item because I very rarely carry a carry-on back. I feel like it is too much to carry and I would rather have the least number of items possible. Typically, I check whatever I can at the front desk of the airport. Loss of luggage has never crossed my mind, I imagine I would be quite upset if I lost luggage but it would not be the end of the world. Not to mention, I do not have to train for a powerlifting competition in effort to take three bags through the airport, so I do not have to wait on my baggage.

I'll be quite honest waiting for baggage can be a chore sometimes. Essentially, the only thing you have is patience and awareness. As the carousel goes around you wait to see if your bag comes around. It's also interesting that luggage being the popular product it is, you will often see people who have the same baggage or luggage as you. I have even heard people taking a suitcase, getting to their hotel and opening it to find out that the luggage they claimed did not belong to them. Now they have to hope that there is some identification so that they can get the baggage to the right person. Or maybe you have been in a situation in which someone has mistakenly taken your luggage, this is why it is imperative that we use the name tag to identify the bag, so that just in case our eyes play a trick on us we can still go about our due diligence and get the back to the right people.

Then there are people like my mom, she is truly a person that leaves room for no mistakes, so she will definitely check a bag, but she will have a filled purse, carry on and personal item. My mother has never had an issue with her luggage, but there it is a journey getting from the ticketing counter through security to the gate because she is carrying so many bags.

Then there are the times we lose luggage. When this happens on vacation or even a business trip it is certainly a frustrating feeling. Many airline companies typically have vouchers for the mistakes that they make when it comes to losing luggage. Statistics show that on average airlines lose about 3 bags per 1,000 passengers. Based on numbers that is not a lot, nonetheless when your luggage is lost it can be a nightmare. Also, know that it is not technically lost until it has been lost for twenty-one days or more. Up until then it is temporarily misplaced, yet if all your trousers and neckties were in your suitcase hopefully you can find the nearest Jos. A Bank in effort to be dressed accordingly.

Life works in a similar way. Some people have traveled light through life, but the issue is they have left all their baggage in the laps of other people. Have you ever met someone who came into your life and when they departed you had more problems that you had before they arrived? This happens in ministry, a person arrives and it seems as if they are a blessing to the work, and they are so talented we have not done our due diligence and looked for things that could be a hinderance. Nonetheless after the honeymoon period wears off, you find out the obstacle in this person's life is not the task in front of them but the baggage they have not unpacked in effort to move forward and walk in purpose. Baggage and insecurities prohibit us from growing and moving at a pace that God intended us to move at. It was interesting to note that Saul had a lot of baggage which caused him to make several irrational decisions.

Irrational decisions that included disobedience and envy driven choices that tainted his legacy as a king of God's people. Insecurity is a big bag to carry, the Bible says, "There was not a more handsome person than he among the children of Israel. From his shoulders upward he was taller than any of the people." Baggage and insecurities are not dependent on good looks, height, or career advancement; it is something that is literally between you and the mirror. As we move through the story, Saul did not believe he had enough to bring to the table. Often times we are the same way, we are on the brink of being chosen but we are looking back at our past, looking back at our life, looking around our room of mistakes and failures and believe we have nothing to bring to the table. Nonetheless, no matter how light you pack, as long as you have a ticket you can get to the destination. Sometimes God does not give us a lot to pack with because He has everything we need when we get to the destination.

You Have Everything You Need

Whether you know it or not, God has been preparing you for this journey for a long time. I remember graduating from college and unsure about the direction of my life. I spoke with a friend who is a principal at a very prominent high school in the Dallas, Texas area and he said, "There is something you have been doing since childhood that has prepared you for purpose. He began his career in education as a chemistry teacher, he had passed up positions with the FDA and the USDA in effort to teach high schoolers elements and chemical compounds. He told me that he had been helping people with things like homework and schoolwork since he was young. That was absolutely true, because I called him in college when I was failing chemistry. He found his purpose early, now I know that does not pan out for everyone, nonetheless when you figure it out hold on to it through all circumstances. Finding purpose and finding happiness are not the same, but if you find purpose you will find joy in every situation.

It was in that moment I realized that helping with VBS, preaching my first sermon at seven years old at Trinity Park Church of Christ and attending youth events and speaking in front of crowds was all God preparing me for my purpose. There is a moment in life in which you realize that every defeat, disappointment, and delay is all preparing you for a purpose driven moment. David's family saw him as a shepherd but what God was doing in that pasture was preparing him to be the Pastor of Israel. There is something that God is doing in your life right now that is preparing you for purpose. Take chances, Goliath might be standing in your way, you may make horrendous mistakes such as engaging the Bathsheba's, and covering it up with the Uriah's of the world but remember Nathan is coming not only to hold you accountable but to remind you of the purpose that God has put on your life. Moses was an older man when God allowed him to walk in his purpose. Who would have thought that an elderly man guilty of murder would lead people out of bondage?

It is important that we know that society does not choose leaders, God does. You may not be society's choice, but as long as you are God's choice that is all that matters and if God has granted you the ability to stand in a leadership role, embrace it because He picked you to lead this team to victory. Even if you do not get to carry out everything you dreamt of, remember the altar has importance in the house of God even if you do not get to build the temple that it sits in. God provides us with expertise and skill similar to what He did for Shamgar, who would have thought an ox goad would preserve an entire nation, nonetheless Shamgar used what he had rather than using armor that he had not tested.

Understand that the ox goad is not mentioned much, let alone the fact that Shamgar is only mentioned twice in the Bible. Just because your story is short does not mean your legacy will not be long.

Shamgar is a short story but has a heavy impact! Six hundred men were destroyed because a farmer used what God gave him. Now he is etched in history forever. A farmer who became a judge because he used what God gave him.

People know who you are by what you use in your hand. Shamgar a farmer with an ox goad because a warrior and savior of a nation. Shamgar is not a warrior complacent with being a farmer but a farmer called to be a warrior. Stop using external factors as an excuse to refrain from being great. Shamgar could have said, "God all I have is an ox goad." It does not matter what you have, it is about who gave it to you. Philistines prohibited people from having weapons specifically Israelites from having weapons. 1 Samuel 13:19, "Now no blacksmith could be found in all the land of Israel, for the Philistines said, Otherwise the Hebrews will make swords or spears." Even in this text, they did not have weaponry, but Jonathan is still victorious because they used what God had given them. Verse 22 says, "So it came about on the day of battle that neither sword nor spear was found in the hands of any of the people who were with Saul and Jonathan, but they were found with Saul and his son Jonathan." It's not about the tools, it's about how the leaders empower the people to use the tool! As black men we should understand this more than anyone else in this country. Our ancestors were forbidden from voting, reading, having jobs; nonetheless they persevered with what they had. Oppression can lead to further oppression or resourcefulness depending on how you use what God has given you. Who among us is going to be the farmer turned warrior or will we continue to be a bunch of warriors okay with being a farmer?

How long will you use excuses, looking at what is in the hands of your neighbor rather than using what is in your hand! A staff is just a walking stick, but a staff in the hands of Moses led people out of Israel. Gopher wood and a hammer are just supplies for a construction worker, but in the hands of Noah it built an ark to save his family. A sling shot and some rocks is an insurance claim waiting to happen in my neighborhood, but in the hands of David is it a king that slayed the Philistine Giant! An ox goad is tool to dig up roots and steer oxen in the right direction but in the hands of Shamgar it was used to destroy the Philistine army! Praise God that nails in our hands and feet are only a tetanus shot but in the hands of Jesus brought salvation unto the entire world.

Moses stood before Pharaoh before the task of a forty-year journey began. Sometimes, the first step can be the most daunting, but it is necessary in effort to move toward the blessings that God has provided for you. Sometimes, God does not want us to ask Pharaoh for a seat, but to stand flat footed in front of his throne and make demands based on the strength of God. One thing we have to be reminded of is the fact that Moses had access, but didn't necessarily feel gifted enough to make demands in the house he was raised in. If we are going to affect change, we need people who can walk in fearlessness. We need access and charisma to move people forward with God. When we are pushed past our limits, know that God has resources for the overtime you are putting in. Moses thought he would fail, but that's what fear does, it makes you think failure is eminent, but faith helps you understand that failure is not an option. God is the I AM resource! Whatever you need...I AM!

Epilogue

How did we get here? How did I write a book? I'll tell you, I was sitting by a preacher I highly regard as a big brother a month after I had been fired from my first ministry work, and telling the story to a table to fellow preachers. He quietly looks over at me and says "Man you should write a book about this." I laughed thinking that it was joke, but my big brother was extremely serious, he even said he was serious. I had this journal that was titled, "Thoughts Become Things." This book is a thing that I never dreamed I would do, if you know me, you probably suggested a hip-hop album would come first, but this is has been the effect of a leadership team and a congregation right here in Ohio providing me with space to be heard and focus on the calling that God has on my life.

I remember living in Phoenix, teaching middle school, teaching midweek bible study, preaching two services on Sunday, experiencing high blood pressure and panic attacks looking for some resolve and God knew just were I would find it. If it was not for the support of my loving congregation that supports my family like we have been family since day one, I do not know if I could do this. It is quite interesting how effective you can be when you have people around you that want the best for you and appreciate the idea of being teammates rather than spectators. I wrote this book for every leader that is struggling with balance right now, and has reached a breaking point not knowing that they have been broken for a long time and God is ready to provide you with support to be effective and diligent within the calling that He put on your life. My therapist constantly reminded me that HIS burden is easy, and His yoke is light. I just had to remember that some things are just not meant for us to carry. So, as you finish this book I ask that you reflect on what you are carrying and know that it is okay to put some stuff down so you can carry the calling that God has instructed you to carry. It is my prayer that you no longer carry resentment, guilt, obligation, and stress but you begin to carry the things that matter most!

About the Author

Vince Ford II is a preacher, activist, teacher, and community leader right here in Columbus, Ohio. Originally from Garland, Texas, Vince is a graduate of Southwestern Christian College and Stephen F. Austin University. He is currently the Senior Minister at the Church of Christ at Genesee Avenue and has served in ministry for over ten years in Nacogdoches, Texas, Phoenix, Arizona, and now Columbus, Ohio. Vince is also the Director of Outreach for Foundations for Families 501(c)(3).

Vince is the founder of Man Up and Educate, a mentoring program serving young men in the Columbus City School District. Vince and his wife Antwanelle have three wonderful sons!

References

New American Standard Bible: 1995 update. (1995). (1 Sa 18:11–12). La Habra, CA: The Lockman Foundation.

New American Standard Bible: 1995 update. (1995). (1 Sa 16:14–19). La Habra, CA: The Lockman Foundation.

The New King James Version. (1982). (Ex 32:31–32). Nashville: Thomas Nelson.

The New King James Version. (1982). (1 Sa 17:28). Nashville: Thomas Nelson.

The New King James Version. (1982). (Ps 5:8). Nashville: Thomas Nelson.

The New King James Version. (1982). (1 Sa 17:34–35). Nashville: Thomas Nelson.

The New King James Version. (1982). (1 Sa 17:37). Nashville: Thomas Nelson.

The New King James Version. (1982). (1 Sa 17:38–39). Nashville: Thomas Nelson.

The New King James Version. (1982). (1 Sa 18:7–8). Nashville: Thomas Nelson.

The New King James Version. (1982). (1 Sa 18:10–12). Nashville: Thomas Nelson.

The New King James Version. (1982). (Lk 22:31). Nashville: Thomas Nelson.

The New King James Version. (1982). (1 Sa 17:9). Nashville: Thomas Nelson.

The New King James Version. (1982). (1 Sa 17:51). Nashville: Thomas Nelson.

The New King James Version. (1982). (Ex 15:2–3). Nashville: Thomas Nelson.

The New King James Version. (1982). (1 Sa 17:26). Nashville: Thomas Nelson.

The New King James Version. (1982). (1 Sa 17:28). Nashville: Thomas Nelson.

The New King James Version. (1982). (1 Sa 17:29–30). Nashville: Thomas Nelson.

The New King James Version. (1982). (Ro 8:28). Nashville: Thomas Nelson.

Brannan, R., & Loken, I. (2014). *The Lexham Textual Notes on the Bible* (Ro 8:28). Bellingham, WA: Lexham Press.

The New King James Version. (1982). (Ps 34:4). Nashville: Thomas Nelson.

The New King James Version. (1982). (2 Sa 11:1). Nashville: Thomas Nelson.

The New King James Version. (1982). (2 Sa 11:2). Nashville: Thomas Nelson.

The New King James Version. (1982). (2 Sa 12:13–14). Nashville: Thomas Nelson.